MILLION DOLLAR MEETINGS

HOW WE MADE MILLIONS MEETING PEOPLE
AND LEARNING FROM THEM

GLEN GOULD

Table of Contents

Introduction

Let's be honest. Most meetings are a huge time suck. So, it's a big promise to make to tell you that you can have Million Dollar Meetings. But stick with me here, because like many things in life, you can't judge a book by its cover, or its title in this case.

What I can promise you is this. Using what I learned, who I met, and the infrastructure of various chambers of commerce, I (along with my family) have generated several million dollars over the ten-plus years I've been involved in chambers. And every dollar can be traced back to a meeting.

Perhaps it wasn't always a sit-down meeting, but it was a meeting nonetheless. Some were chance meetings at a business-after-hours event, some were at luncheons, and some were committee meetings or other non-networking specific events. And they all add up.

I guarantee that you can duplicate what I've done. You too can have Million Dollar Meetings.

And if you're looking for a big hit, here it is. My wife once met someone at a chamber event and within 30 days had landed a piece of business that has meant over $1 million to our company.

Honestly, she isn't a trained networker. She probably hasn't attended 10 formal networking events in her entire life. But she does have the ability to meet people, find them interesting, and learn how she can help them solve a problem they have. I bet you have that ability as well, and if you don't, you'll find help for that in this book too.

And just because I've focused on our experiences in chambers of commerce, don't think these tips and techniques won't work outside of them. What you'll learn in this book can be applied to any group or organization. Anywhere where people gather, including associations, church groups, civic groups, or even unions. This is about how people interact, not specifically where they do.

So, yes, you can have your own Million Dollar Meetings.

If you're expecting a book telling you that everything we did to bring us success was due to our chamber membership, you're going to be disappointed—slightly.

You see, we did a lot of hard, heavy lifting and strategic work to generate over two million dollars in revenue, and that was with an average ticket of less than $30!

But what we learned, who we met, and how we utilized our chamber membership was essential to our success. And that's what is most important to understand as we outline what we did, how we did it, and also what worked and didn't work so you can successfully guide your business past the seven-figure mark.

But don't be fooled. It isn't easy. Simple? Yes. But not easy. It will take work. But something tells me you're not afraid of a little hard work. After all, you've launched your own business, even if that business sells its services to one company (what most people call a job), and that makes us kindred spirits. We like to make good things happen.

It is my sincere hope that you will find success, fulfillment, and joy in your enterprise. And if this book can make the journey a bit easier, that would delight me.

Are you ready to make the leap to seven figures? Let's go!

CHAPTER 1
A useful tool

First, a full disclosure.

It won't take you long to discover I'm a chamber guy. Yep, I worked in and with chambers of commerce for ten years. My path wasn't normal. After a failed short stint as a member in my first chamber, I waited a few years before I tried again. Like so many, I had a bad experience my first go-round.

And that's why I'm writing this book. You see, I know from firsthand experience and from the success stories of hundreds of people I have met that a chamber of commerce membership is a powerful tool when placed in the proper hands and used correctly.

My second experience as a member benefited me so much. I volunteered (more about the value of that later), served on the board, and ultimately became the president, a paid position of the chamber. After a year, I became the director of small to mid-sized business at the Metro

Atlanta Chamber, one of the nation's largest. After four years, I became the vice president of the Newnan-Coweta Chamber, the 2015 National Chamber of the Year.

Ben Turpin and me during a presentation for the International Special Events Society

All the while, my business partner Ben Turpin and I traveled the country, training chambers and their staffs on what we'd learned. And the more we trained, the more we learned. It was a great experience.

So, you might think that I'm a conspirator and that this book is nothing but a propaganda piece for the chamber industry. Read on and I think you'll find that is not the case. I'm a believer in the opportunity for you and your business to grow using a chamber of commerce. And while some chambers do a better job than others of facilitating that growth, for the most part, chambers miss the mark.

And they should miss the mark. It's taken me a long time to come to grips with the idea that today's chamber of commerce, roughly defined as "house of business," isn't equipped to build businesses. It is equipped to facilitate growth, and I'm a firm believer in using every tool at your disposal to achieve your personal and business goals, so long as it isn't illegal or immoral, as my mother would say.

My dream is that each chamber would be staffed with cutting-edge, knowledgeable business experts whose sole job is to solve business problems for local businesses. But that would put many business coaches and universities out of work and would cost far more than the average business would be willing to pay.

So, for now, the local chamber is a tool. A useful tool. But no tool works without an operator. That's your job.

CHAPTER 2

How to use this book

If you're like me, you want to get to the point. Just the facts, please. I understand. But many people find it hard to embrace "just the facts" without the backstory and context. In this book, you'll find both.

If you desire "just the facts" and wish to move quickly through the lessons, just look for the bold **"Here's what I learned," "Here's what I did," "Here's what to do," "Here's what not to do,"** and **"POWER TIP"** sections. But should you do that, you may miss out on some valuable context that will make the process easier to understand and implement.

If, on the other hand, you like the backstory and context, read on. I've done my best to tell stories that enhance the lessons I've learned. When it applies—or more likely, when I can remember— I've included the names of people and their companies who were instrumental in providing the lessons I learned and implemented that ultimately resulted in seven figures through my chamber membership.

And one more thing. I'll use "me," "I," "we," and "us" interchangeably because, while our family built this business through our chamber membership, much of the chamber experience was my own. I'll also use "customer" and "client" interchangeably because most people are seeking "customers," and we call our customers "clients."

My family

CHAPTER 3

How it Began for Me

I joined my first chamber, which was a business association at the time, in 1999. But it wasn't by choice.

Bill Woodman (I've changed his name) came to my wife's business one day. She and my sister-in-law had opened a small shop called Artistic Accents in downtown Punta Gorda, Florida. They bought used furniture, painted or otherwise embellished it, and then resold the items.

Newspaper clipping from Sarasota-Herald Tribune, 1998

Bill stopped by in a dual capacity. He not only ran the local business association, but he also had an article once a week in the local newspaper profiling a local business. Bill told us, "I can make you or break you in this town." We wanted to "be made" and didn't want him to "break us," so we joined the business association, got an article profiling our business in the paper, and that was about it. Nothing happened.

Here's what I learned: This was a big lesson for me. Like most people, I thought joining the local chamber or business association was enough. And getting a profile in the local paper? Well, how much business could we handle? We never found out. The crowds didn't come, the phone didn't ring, and the cash register sounded more like crickets than cha-ching. We closed in less than six months and of course left the business association as a result.

Here's (more of) what I learned: Turns out, this is the first of many lessons I learned from chamber membership. Joining does very little to improve your business if you don't use what you've learned. But before you begin to believe this is a retread of the same old "use it or lose it" mantra, stick around a while. You'll soon see it is not. While you have to "use it or lose it," you might just find as I have that you can use something in a different way than it was intended and get a result that is quite unexpected—and wonderful.

Here's what I did: I use this lesson every day in my business. In everything I do, I remember that just being in business isn't enough. I have to do all I can to make my business stand out. No one will understand what my business is all about or what it can do for them if I don't first clearly understand those things and how to articulate them to the client. There isn't "one thing" I can do that will make all the difference. It takes a multifaceted effort. And I remember that no one person can make me or break me except me.

Here's what to do: Take a quick walk (virtually) around your business. Are you relying too much on one thing, one person, one promotion, or circumstances you don't control to make you or break you? Look hard at what you're doing. Is there something you've learned in the past that you can leverage differently in your current business? Do you have a clear understanding of what you and your business are about and know how to explain that to others, including customers, in a way that is easy for them to understand and appreciate? Are you really doing all you can? Here's a hint: No, you're not, and neither am I. But we can always strive to do just a bit more that will make all the difference.

Sadly, chamber people have a tendency to overvalue and overpromise their product and results. It's natural. They believe what they are saying because they've seen it work for a few people, so they know it can work for you. But what they fail to see is *why* it doesn't work *when* it doesn't work for people. Chamber people find a good reason for failures.

"They didn't come" or "They didn't get involved," they'll say. What they fail to realize is that coming to events and getting involved is only part of what is needed to successfully grow your business to seven figures and beyond through chamber membership.

And for those people who never see the value and never join, chamber people have an explanation for that as well. "They just don't understand all that we do. They don't get the value."

Here's what I learned: It's not just "chamber people" who overpromise and overvalue their products or services. I learned that I do it too. It's my obligation to promote my products and services to the right client so they can enjoy the benefits they desire. But it's also my obligation to not overpromise to the point I cannot live up to expectations.

Here's what I did: I examined and continue to examine everything we do and say to ensure we aren't, purposely or not, creating an expectation we cannot fulfill in the minds of our clients and prospects. I am reminded daily that it is my job to ensure everyone who works for and with our company understands what to say and not to say to a client or vendor.

And when it comes to marketing or advertising, we are super vigilant to ensure what we say and imply is congruent with our Statement of Value (more on that later). A simple example is how we answer the phone. "Good morning, this is Glen speaking. How may I serve you?" Another is our email closing. "Thank you for the opportunity to serve." You see, our entire focus is on service. At Dry Cleaning Connection, our family's dry cleaning pickup and delivery business, our entire focus is on the client experience. Not on dry cleaning. We're not even dry cleaners. We're in the personal services business, which means we have very few if any competitors.

End cap of a video advertisement for Dry Cleaning Connection

Here's what to do: Examine everything you have in print. Listen to what you and your employees say to clients and vendors. Write it down. Take time to analyze what you are saying and what you are implying. Then, decide what you wish to say and imply. We'll cover more on this later, but don't wait until tomorrow to begin clarifying your message today. Anytime a prospective client doesn't understand what you do or the value you provide, it is your fault, not theirs. You are the one who failed to properly position your product or service and educate others about it.

That lesson alone could be worth a million dollars or more to the right person with the right product or service that solves the problem(s) of the right client(s).

Why do so many overvalue their product or service? We believe. That's really all there is to it. We believe, and we're so familiar with our products or services that we can't help but overhype them.

In the chamber business, when you're selling a membership that can have tremendous value for less than a cup of coffee (and I mean home-brewed) per day, how much can it take to make it a great value?

The problem is, chamber people relate to the financial investment but fail to understand the intangible cost of time invested. They don't understand that there is a real cost to time, and an opportunity cost for what could have been done rather than getting involved in a chamber event or initiative.

Here's what I learned: Price, the amount someone pays for a product or service, is a one-time thing. Usually it is determined by the amount of money paid. Cost, on the other hand, is a lifetime thing. It is determined by the price paid versus the value received. Too often we focus on price and fail to recognize the cost.

Here's what I did: I describe this in full later, but I determined how much it would cost me to gain new customers through a chamber experience and then decided to pay that price in advance. Later in business, I've priced products and services not by the price a competitor might charge but by the value the customer receives. This almost always results in higher margins and happier customers.

Here's what to do: Look back at what you charge for your products and services. How did you determine what to charge? Chances are you've priced things based on what you think the market will bear, and that is almost always determined by what your competitors charge. What value does your customer get by buying from you? What is the real cost they pay, not the price they pay? Here's a hint: Raise your prices.

Now you understand the difference between price and cost. A chamber membership may have a price of a few hundred dollars, but the real cost to join and get involved is much higher.

> **POWER TIP:** If it isn't profitable, don't do it. But remember, profit is often a delayed result.

That's important to remember. Many highly profitable activities become profitable only after an extended period of time. So yes, I suggest you go to chamber events. I suggest you get involved in a chamber initiative. I suggest you volunteer when you can. But I also suggest you remember the cost of doing so. Make your investment pay.

And here's really great news. I'll show you how to make it pay in ways other than the direct investment of your time versus the return on that investment. I'll show you how to build social capital, how to cross-appropriate ideas from one industry to another, and how to build trust and expert status, all while using your chamber membership to leverage it all.

Seven figures through chamber membership is not an unrealistic number. I've done it. Many others have too. Now it's your turn.

I'm going to break this down into activities you might engage in at stages during your chamber journey. I don't know, but it just seems easier to think about beginning, middle, and end. And yes, an end game should be thought out for your chamber journey.

Every super-successful chamber member will eventually burn out. Either by the repetitive nature of chamber life or by working their way from new member to past board chair, everyone finds that chamber membership, like an airplane flight, has a takeoff, cruising, and landing. While I've had my own trip through the chamber (several times in several locations), I'm going to include some things I didn't do but that I witnessed or learned about firsthand. If it works, it's included. And if it doesn't work, it's included as well with a warning not to try it.

CHAPTER 4

Begin with a plan

You might think the first thing to do is join a chamber. But let's hold on a bit. Even if you're already a member and you're looking for a way to use your chamber membership to grow your business to seven figures, now is a good time to start over with a plan.

So, before you join or re-engage, let's take a look at what you expect from your membership and involvement.

In picking up this book, you may be hoping to build your business to seven figures. That requires a completely different strategy than building your public presence. So, what is it that you hope to gain through your chamber membership? Most people will say, "I want a fatter wallet." In fact, most people would be happy if they could just invest $500 and get at least $501 back. That's a very shortsighted approach.

You need to be able to measure your success, and to

do so, you'll need a specific result in mind. You should be seeking more. Here are some ideas:

- Build my business to seven figures or more

- Become a recognized brand or person in the local community

- Give back to the community

- Develop friendships

- Network with other business professionals

- Attend educational programming

- Better understand the local economy

- Be "in the know"

- Develop leadership skills

- Get involved in local politics

- Become board chair

The list is really endless, and the possibilities are as well. You need to decide what you want from your chamber experience. And that should drive all your decisions when it comes to using your membership.

As for me, I wanted to grow my business. I didn't think of growing it to seven figures initially. I had a simple equation. I wanted to recruit in one year new clients who had an annual value of ten times the investment of dollars and time.

This brings up a new lesson I learned at the chamber. Someone, somewhere recommended I read *The E-Myth* by Michael Gerber. I strongly recommend it to you if you haven't read it yet.

In essence, Gerber suggests that you can value your time only in an equal amount to the value you would pay someone else to do a task for you. In other words, if you'd pay a salesperson 25 percent commission, your time selling is worth exactly that.

For me, I imagined I was a commissioned salesperson for my company when I attended chamber events. I didn't have a base, so I ate only when I sold. But when I did, it was worth 25 percent of the sale.

You have to know your numbers. In my business, a typical client is worth $600 a year, and they stick for five years. Here's the math for successful chamber membership as I outlined it in the beginning.

If I invest $500, I need to be able to trace back $5,000 in sales to make it worth my while. To get $5,000, I'd need to sell 12 new clients directly through my chamber experience. $600 per year x 12 = $7,200. $7,200 x .25 (commission) = $1,800. $7,200 - $1,800 = $5,400 or just over 10 x my investment.

That's what I thought I would need to feel like my investment of time and money was successful. I got a whole lot more, but we'll discuss that in later sections.

What about you? What will it take for you to feel your investment of time and dollars was worth it? Really think about this. After all, would you invest in inventory without a plan to profit from selling it?

Don't do this halfheartedly. Have a goal. While I learned this before my chamber experience, it is worth repeating here: The difference between successful people and those who are unsuccessful is that successful people have goals. I'm not sure who said it first, but I am sure I didn't.

Now you have a goal. What's next?

CHAPTER 5

Identify your Ideal Customer

Here's what I learned: Another lesson I learned that has paid me an untold fortune is you have to know who your target client or customer is. I learned it from Kathy Lehner in Venice, Florida. Kathy is a Realtor turned chamber executive, and someone who changed my life for the better fifteen years ago.

I had recently joined the Venice Area Chamber of Commerce because I wanted to grow my business in a new community. I had a few friends and knew Kathy from Toastmasters. She suggested I join, and she met me at the door for the first event I attended.

She greeted me with a big smile, a handshake, and a question I'll never forget. "Who do you need to meet?" she asked.

I'll never forget it because it was the last time I didn't have an answer. I had never thought of knowing in advance who I wanted or needed to meet. I didn't even have a target customer in mind. I was speechless.

Thankfully, Kathy knew just what to do. She began introducing me to people she knew would welcome me and get me talking. That's the first step to being involved. You have to start talking to people and have them talk to you.

Here's what I did: I was lucky. I eventually stumbled onto the solution. I found that asking questions was the first step. I began by asking others their name and eventually got to asking them what they do, how they started doing it, and what they like about what they do. I found that asking some personal questions worked too. So I'd ask them what they do for fun, or the best restaurant in town, or if they have family in the area.

Here's what not to do: Don't ask if they're married, or if they have a wife or husband. Families take all shapes and forms these days. This goes for meeting people in any environment.

Remember, it's easier to meet the type of people you want to meet, or even be introduced to them, if you know who they are and can tell others who you are looking for. Here's a couple of ideas for how to determine who you need to meet and to explain to others who they are.

Here's what I did: I began thinking of people I'd like to work with. I also thought about my favorite customers in the past and what I liked about them.

Here's what I learned: I learned that Rick Warren of Saddleback Church had an ideal member profile. They even called them "Saddleback Sam and Sally." I used that idea to narrow down my best client and gave them names. Using the idea of an Ideal Client and the idea of a nondesired client, I eventually developed my imaginary firing spree and locked on to exactly what I wanted.

Here's what to do: First, have what I call an imaginary firing spree. Imagine for a moment that you are going to fire every customer you have except one, with the understanding that every customer you ever get in the future will be just like the one you kept.

The Imaginary Firing Spree:

- Who would you keep?
- The fastest paying?
- The biggest revenue?

- The easiest to please?
- The most connected?
- Some other criteria?

Who would you keep? This is important because it will be the basis of who you will be looking for and who you will tell others you are looking for.

Now, how would you describe that person?

Is he or she well known, and therefore you could just mention their name? I would like to be introduced to (person's name).

What are the characteristics of your ideal customer? (It's OK to use these as characteristics, just don't ask them of people.)

- Married?
- Single?
- Children?

Other characteristics they may have:

- Sports enthusiast?
- Educator?
- Business owner?
- Neighborhood they live in?

The list of characteristics is limitless. What could you say about your ideal customer that would identify him or her to others?

Before you move on, clearly identify the characteristics of a nondesired client as well. There will be people you won't want to work with, and you don't want to accidentally attract them into your business. Don't focus on the negative too long, and don't make it too restrictive, or you'll lock out some potential winners. Just be sure to know who you don't want too.

If you are starting out and you can't do the imaginary firing spree, you're going to have to make some assumptions. But if you're just starting out, you have hopefully begun to know the types of people who your product or service will help the most.

Try this acronym that will lead you to the characteristics of your ideal customer.

T – Title: What title does your ideal customer hold? Sales Manager, Company Owner, etc.

A – Association: Who do they associate with? Golf buddies, in civic clubs, etc.

N – Name: Actual name of the person or company they work for: Bob Smith, Coca-Cola, etc.

Remember, you can be on the beach getting a **TAN** if

you just focus on clearly identifying your ideal customer and learning how to contact them through others.

Here's what I did (and still do): After the embarrassment of not knowing who I needed to meet, I started writing down the names and titles of people I did need to meet. I constantly identify the ideal client I could have. I keep her in my mind. I write down her characteristics. I'm certain to know how to describe her. And that description is always changing, so I have to keep on top of it.

Here's what I learned: Being in a chamber exposes you to people you normally wouldn't be associating with. You'll be in contact with new people who have new experiences and new ideas. You can't help but find new opportunities when you're around new people with new ideas or ideas that are foreign to you or your industry.

Here's what to do: Before you go any further, take a moment to write down your ideal customer. Don't worry. Before long, your ideal customer will change, and so will your business. It's very common. We can see only what is within our reach. As you and your company grow, you'll find all sorts of possibilities you didn't see just a few short months earlier.

CHAPTER 6

Create your Statement of Value

Ok, so now you've identified your ideal customer. Now what?

Here's what I learned: You have to be able to explain to someone exactly what it is that makes you, your product, service, or offering singularly different and better than anyone else's. Ryan Deiss of DigitalMarketer.com calls this a Statement of Value.

Here's what to do: Develop your Statement of Value

For our business, we enable busy people to experience greater control and freedom in their lives by picking up and delivering dry cleaning at their home or office.

That's our Statement of Value. That's what I'll tell people who ask what we do.

Now identify your Statement of Value. What do you enable your ideal client to experience?

Now that you know your Statement of Value, how would you tie that to your ideal customer to make it simple for people to remember and share?

Here's what to do: Narrow down your ideal customer to one simple sentence that is easy for others to remember and hard for you to forget. This is your Ideal Customer Identity.

For us, our ideal client is a family with dual incomes with one traveling into the city to work. They have school-age children, and they live in a $400K-plus home. That's our Ideal Customer Identity.

How would you describe your ideal customer? What are the characteristics you outlined above? What is your Ideal Customer Identity? Put that into a simple sentence.

Here's what to do: Identify who might be connected to your ideal client. This is the answer to "Who do you need to meet?"

CHAPTER 7

Create an Ideal Client Association List

It might seem odd, but you really don't want to meet your ideal client right away every time. Sometimes it is best to have an introduction from someone your ideal client already has a relationship with.

If I had thought out the answer to "Who do you need to meet?" and had told Kathy I needed to meet my ideal client (e.g., a family with dual incomes with one traveling into the city to work, school-age children, and lives in a $400K-plus home), she might have been hard-pressed to introduce me to anyone.

Here's what I learned: People at chamber events want to help you. That's the good news. The bad news is, if you haven't explained to them how to help you properly, you'll likely get a slew of bad leads and referrals. That's because people want to help so much they'll try to make a connection even when one isn't there. It's normal.

You have to set the stage to get the best possible outcome. After identifying who is connected to your ideal client, along with your Statement of Value and your Ideal Customer Identity, you'll be more likely to make the right connection.

Here's what not to do: Never, never, never use the word "anybody" or a similar word when describing your Ideal Customer Identity. Nobody knows any-body. Be specific.

Here's what to do: Grab a pen and pad of paper. There's something that happens between your thoughts and writing them down that is magical, so go ahead, do it old school. Write down your Ideal Customer Identity at the top. Then, begin to think of all the people who associate with your Ideal Cus-tomer Identity.

For us, we easily thought of clothing stores, shoe stores, alteration shops, and linen stores since we're in the dry cleaning business. But a little more thought revealed:

- Lawn and landscape services
- Window cleaners
- Maid services
- Pest control services

- Internet providers
- Pool services
- Painters
- Siding companies
- Pressure washing services
- Fence installers
- Alarm companies
- Electricians
- Plumbers
- Septic services
- Audiovisual installers
- Electronics sellers
- Furniture stores
- Rug stores
- Carpet cleaners
- Remodelers
- Bath tub refinishers
- Appliance installers and sellers
- Automobile dealers
- Auto repair
- Home delivery services
- Pizza and other food delivery

You'd think we'd just about covered it until we remembered our customers are people, not just houses. Then we thought of:

- Hairstylists
- Personal trainers

- Nutritionists
- Healthcare providers
- Custom clothiers that come to your home
- Entertainment venues
- Private schools
- Preschools and day care
- Children's sports teams
- Adult sports
- Gyms and health clubs
- Restaurants
- Movie theatres

Essentially anywhere our ideal customer might spend time or money is somewhere a connection might exist.

Spend some time on this list. Keep it handy because you'll come up with new ideas all the time. Write them down and revisit the list often. This is your Ideal Customer Association List. Once you have a list, you can pick one item from the list any time you attend an event.

Here's what to do: When someone asks you, "Who do you need to meet?" simply pull one or two from your Ideal Client Association List and mention them. As you attend more events, you'll begin to realize where and when the people on your list will be attending, making it that much easier to be introduced.

For now, simply choose no more than two and run with them. For us, that might be, "I'd like to be introduced to heads of private schools and preschools." A few months ago, I was interested in meeting lawn service and maid service providers. Change it to keep it fresh, but keep it consistent long enough for people to really hear you. It may take telling someone 5-7 times before he or she will understand what you're looking for and make an introduction that makes you a fortune. Stick with it until you hear people asking you to change that introduction. You'll know it's time when people start asking you if people other than the ones you're asking for might be a fit. For example, if you're asking to meet hairstylists and people start asking if you want to meet the owner of a nail salon, you can bet they understand you want hairstylists. They've just moved on to the next logical level, and so should you.

> **Here's what I learned:** When you put together your Statement of Value, Ideal Customer Identity, and your Ideal Customer Association List, you'll be prepared to answer virtually any question you may be asked at any time with confidence and clarity.

> **Here's what I did:** I committed to paper and memory our Statement of Value, Ideal Customer Identity, and Ideal Customer Association List. I refer back to it almost daily.

> **Here's what to do:** Write down and memorize your

Statement of Value, Ideal Customer Identity, and Ideal Customer Association List and refer to it daily. Make changes as you and your company change.

Now, you're ready to join a chamber.

What? All this work and you're just now ready to join? How can that be?

Remember, you bought this book to take a shortcut to using a chamber membership to get to seven figures in your business. I used everything mentioned so far in this book to make seven figures through my chamber membership. But I learned the hard way through trial, error, and time. You don't have to unless that's your thing. But somehow, I think it's not. So as I said, now you're ready to join a chamber.

CHAPTER 8

Joining a Chamber

If you live in a small community, you'll have an easy time choosing a chamber. That's because there will likely be only one. But if you live in a community with more than one chamber, you're going to need to do a bit of homework. This is the first of many places your work in setting a goal for your membership will pay off.

There's a saying in the chamber business: "If you've seen one chamber, you've seen one chamber." The idea is that each chamber is so unique, if you compare them, you'll see very little in common. I disagree.

I do agree, however, that one chamber may be a better opportunity than another depending on your goal or goals.

Usually chambers are geographically specific. Their service area and reach are limited to a specific geographic area. That means they attract people from that area as well. If you want to expand into a new geographic area, joining and getting involved in the chamber in that area is a great way to expand before you put down roots.

I joined the local chamber first. Then, when I had established myself and my company locally and wanted to expand, I joined the neighboring chamber as well. There's a lot to know about being involved in two chambers at the same time.

> **Here's what not to do:** While this book doesn't cover it in detail, here's one thing to avoid: Never give a referral to two different referral partners. You might be tempted to refer a friend or colleague to someone in your local chamber, and then when you meet a different service provider in a neighboring chamber, you might want to make an impression by giving that same referral to her. Don't do it. For more tips like this, download my free ebook at 101NetworkingNuggets.com.

You will likely benefit most by joining the local chamber first. But if you're in a big community or metropolitan area, you might find more than one chamber serving your local area. Now, it's time to find out which one is best.

It's natural to think that bigger is better. After all, if you have a bigger pond, you have more fish, right? But the real question should be, "Which pond has my fish? Which pond is my bait the best in?"

If you're in a business that has a lot of competition, you may find the smaller chamber is better suited to you because it will be easier to stand out in the smaller crowd. On the other hand, if you have the ability to show how you are different, the bigger crowd is always the better opportunity.

Here's what I learned: Joining the right chamber to reach your goals is critical to success. Every chamber does have a unique personality and attracts certain people more easily than others. Chambers are cliquish, and you'll need to know before you join that you're joining the right clique.

Here's what I did: While five chambers serve the geographic area my business serves (actually many more if you include the regional and national chambers), I chose the chamber covering the largest percentage of my current business.

Here's why: By joining and getting involved in the chamber where I already had business, it was easier for me to get plugged in and begin getting referrals fast because I already knew some people, and they already knew me.

Here's what to do: If you are already in business, make sure you leverage the relationships you already have when you join the local chamber. Ask around. You'll be surprised how many people you serve are involved in the chamber. And once they know you want to be a part of what they're a part of, they'll be more excited about continuing to do business with you and telling others about you too!

Here's what else to do: Ask a current customer or a friend who is a member of the chamber to invite you to an event. Believe me, they'll be delighted, and you'll get a much better first impression when you go with someone you know. If your contact is active in the chamber, you'll be accepted right away. If he or she hasn't been active for a while, they'll likely appreciate the excuse to get reacquainted with the chamber. Everyone wins.

If you're new to the area, take a look at the chamber website. Poke around. See what kind of activities they have. Read about their initiatives, what they stand for, and what they say their mission is. Check out their board of directors. Who is on the board? Is one of your competitors on the board?

Here's what you're really looking for. Is this the kind of place I want to hang out at? Are these the kinds of people I can relate to? Are my target clients a part of this group? Does this group believe in what I believe in? Can I buy into their mission?

If you don't know anyone who is a member, call the chamber and ask to speak to someone in sales. Tell them you are interested in what the chamber has to offer, and you'd like to visit before you sign up to be sure it's right for you. They'll always let you come free of charge at least once. But if you talk to someone first and they know you are coming, they will make a few introductions and break the ice for you. They'll want you to have a good time and have a beneficial experience.

Either way, you can be certain to have the best chance to experience the chamber in a good light. Why would you want to do that? Wouldn't you want to see the chamber "warts and all"?

Not really.

Here's what I learned: Expectations influence our experience more than any other single factor. If we expect to have a good time, we usually do. If we expect to profit from an experience or endeavor, we usually do. And if we're with someone we want to be with or someone who wants us to have a good experience, we usually do.

And that's very important. Because you want to have a good first experience to ensure your next experience will be too. I learned that people who have a good first experience usually come back. That's good for business and good for chamber membership.

Here's what I did: In our business, we set the stage for our new clients to expect a good experience. We ask for referrals before we begin service. That way, we subtly tell our customers we expect they'll like us so much they'll want to refer us. We also show we're confident in our results. We provide a series of emails that explain the value we bring, how to use our service, how to refer us, and much more.

The first line in the first message any client receives is, "Thanks for giving our service a try, and I know you are going to love it!"

Here's what to do: Examine the expectation level you're building for your clients through their first experience. As outlined before, don't overpromise, but make sure you show your confidence in the results you'll provide to the point they expect things to be great. When they expect the best, they'll be looking for it and will usually find it!

Once you've done your research and attended an event or two, it's time to take the plunge. It's time to commit and join. Don't make the mistake of attending more than two events without joining. While you may think no one will notice, especially in a larger chamber, trust me, people will. And they will talk.

Here's what I learned: While you'll be amazed how little people think about you, you'll be equally amazed at how much they'll notice when you are being cheap. The staff at one chamber continually mentioned how cheap a member was who had taken extra lunches home five years earlier. He had never done so when I was there, and he was a tireless volunteer. But the staff never forgot.

Even if you aren't intentionally being cheap, if you appear to be, you'll be tagged as such. And being cheap is almost impossible to overcome. No one wants to associate with someone who is cheap, and no one wants to introduce cheap people to other people.

Don't go on the cheap. To paraphrase something I heard from sales training expert Brian Tracy, "Success is promised to those who are willing to pay the price in advance." Chamber membership works the same way. Agree to pay the price in advance and you'll be successful.

OK, I'm ready to pay. But how much should I pay?

Unfortunately, chambers don't always make it easy to understand how much to pay. Here's a brief explanation of the different types of chamber dues memberships.

If you live in Europe, membership in the local chamber is automatic as a part of your business license fees in most cases. In other parts of the world, and especially in the United States, chambers price their memberships in one of two ways: Fair Share or Tiered Dues.

Fair Share: It's ironic that an organization that promotes free enterprise has its basic dues based on what you are able to pay, but that's the case for most chambers in the United States. Fair Share dues were introduced as a way to equitably share the burden of funding the chamber among the members who use it. The thought was, an insurance company with 25 employees is more likely to have someone use the services of the chamber than a small business with 2 employees. While that makes sense, it isn't necessarily "fair."

What's worse, most Fair Share chambers have special fees for certain industries. A motel might pay based on the number of beds they have, or a bank might be charged based on its assets.

To be honest, there's nothing "fair" about the Fair Share model, but that's what it's been called for as long as I've been around the business.

Then someone came up with the brilliant idea that chambers should charge companies in accordance with their use, or desired use, of services provided by the chamber. This is called Tiered Dues.

Each "tier" comes with additional benefits. Some chambers structure their "tiers" to include marketing opportunities and free attendance to paid events. Many "tiers" include a discount for bundling services and paying in advance.

Both the Fair Share and Tiered Dues models have pluses and minuses, but both are designed to serve the chamber first. This is one of many examples where chambers still have not adopted the idea that they must compete for our business in creative ways that benefit us.

While Tiered Dues may provide added benefits, the real purpose of offering them is to ensure that advertising and sponsorship opportunities are sold, chamber events are filled, and the chamber budget is met. They usually aren't thought out in terms of how they benefit the potential member until they've been planned in such a way to ensure the coffers are full.

Here's what I learned: Perhaps I was naïve, but when I first started in the chamber, I took a look at what the companies who spent the most in previous years had spent their money on. Then I proposed a slight increase that included all they had spent on in the past, plus a few new items they hadn't considered. Then I created a new category of member with additional marketing benefits. These were benefits already being offered or benefits that had no additional cost to the chamber. By bundling it all together, I was able to increase the spend from each member and provide greater benefit too.

Here's what I did: We profile a customer's business in our monthly newsletter. Sometimes it includes a coupon or other incentive to recruit new customers. By offering this benefit to our customers, we show we're interested in their success, and we're offering something our competitors can't—exposure to our list of highly qualified prospects.

Here's what to do: Identify things you can do that cost little to nothing but have great value to your customer. What products or services could you include in your offering that could enhance your customer's experience or benefits while costing you little or nothing?

OK, back to deciding how much to pay. If you're joining a Fair Share chamber, the decision will be made for you. It's usually determined by how many employees you have. If you're joining a Tiered Dues chamber, you should carefully look at the benefits offered and determine if you'd pay for them à la carte.

Remember, I told you early on that chamber people seem to have an inflated value of their services. You might find your local chamber values being in the membership list worth $500 or more. They may claim your Google ranking will go up because you're listed on their website. Even if you believe these claims, would you pay for them? Probably not.

But just as they overvalue some things, they'll undervalue others that may matter to you. Getting in front of the right contacts can be extremely valuable, especially once you've identified your Ideal Customer Identity. Don't be confused by believing this can be done simply through advertising. An ad on the chamber website or in the print newsletter is often very expensive as a stand-alone product.

When advertising through a chamber, you should examine the cost of the ad and compare it to the value you'll receive. Steve Stripling with United Bank taught me this in a very simple way.

I was proposing he invest $5,000 in our chamber, and one of the biggest benefits I focused on was all the marketing the bank would receive. Just think of the exposure his bank would enjoy. Their logo on every piece of printed material, the recognition they'd enjoy at events, and the website backlinks would improve their Google search ranking.

Then Steve said, "For $5,000, I can run 1,000 television ads in the local market. Do you really think I'm going to spend $5,000 with you when I can be on TV 1,000 times?"

Here's what I learned: You have to find what the customer values, not what you value, when attracting and keeping customers. Steve didn't value our advertising at the chamber, but he did value the enhanced golf tournament package and access to community leaders through our Enhanced Investors program.

Here's what I did: We are constantly surveying our clients to ensure we really understand what they value, and then we focus on that exclusively in our promotional and marketing materials. You'd think in the dry cleaning business that customers care about price. After all, virtually every dry cleaner runs coupons and multiple-piece specials to attract us to their store. But we've found our customers care very little about price. Don't get me wrong, we have to stay competitive, but we don't need to constantly talk about it.

Here's what to do: Survey your customers to determine what really matters to them. Ask questions like, "Why do you buy from me instead of my competitors?" "How did you choose us?" "What annoys you most about our industry?" "What one thing would you ask me to change?" You can come up with your own set of questions to determine what matters most to your customers, just be careful to not lead them to the answers you want.

One of the best values is narrowing the pool of potential attendees to the right contacts. Whether through special membership levels, volunteer positions and committees, or targeted events that attract your Ideal Customer, there are ways to narrow down the number and types of people at the events you attend to better ensure you're in the right place.

Some chambers have special membership categories that are clearly "pay to play" opportunities. They may be called "Enhanced Investors" or "Board of Advisors" or some other title, but what these memberships should be called is "I paid, so I get to play."

If you can budget it, these memberships can be a tremendous value for you and your company. Not only do they usually come with added marketing, recognition, and prestige, they also come with personal connections with the movers and shakers in the community. Essentially, you can buy your way to connect with the who's who in the business community.

But let's say you cannot spend $1,000 or more to move up to a special membership level. Or let's say you just don't believe that will benefit you enough to justify the investment. Does that mean you're left sifting through all the members to find a few Ideal Customers? Not at all.

There are simple, free, or almost free strategies that I

used, and you can too to ensure you meet the right people first. But let's not get ahead of ourselves. There are a couple of steps you need to take first, not the least of which is joining the chamber.

Before you do, make certain you have a name badge and plenty of business cards. Ideally you'll have a flyer or brochure and other marketing materials as well, but a badge and card will go a long way.

People still expect you to have a business card (if you want to know more about why, you can read a blog post I wrote on the subject at https://goo.gl/JSxT7B).

A name badge makes it easier for people to relate to you. Let's face it, we all meet a lot of people in our day, and we often can't remember their names. It makes us uncomfortable unless the people we meet make it easy for us by wearing a name badge. You want people to feel at ease around you, so wear a badge and take the pressure off them!

What are you waiting for? Go ahead, join! You're ready.

CHAPTER 9

You've joined the chamber. Now what?

Some chambers are better than others in getting you plugged in. But all chambers will have some sort of orientation meeting for you to attend. I know, sounds like the orientation before school each year, and it kind of is. But it is always worth attending, provided you have a plan and know what you are looking for.

Problem is, most chamber orientation meetings are already scheduled at the beginning of the year, and it may be a month, or even a few months, before you can attend one. That won't work. So, I'm going to show you how to get plugged in regardless of the plan to do so your chamber has set.

You should still plan on following your chamber's plan as well if they have one. Many of the steps they will outline are steps I took and will cover here. You'll just be ahead of the game in most cases by following my plan.

CHAPTER 10

Meet the Staff

Every chamber has a staff, even the smallest has a volunteer staff, and you need to be known, liked, and trusted by them.

Most people fail to realize the value a friendship with staff can bring. And most people do what I did at first, start at the top. Of course, you want to know the president and the board chair and members, but my experience left me empty.

Here's what I learned: People don't care about you until they know you care about them. May sound a bit self-centered, but it is true. People care about and think about themselves and what matters to them first, last, and always. Knowing this provides you with insight into building meaningful relationships, not just with the chamber staff but with everyone you meet.

In addition, the most important person to meet

in any organization is the person who greets the most people. In a chamber, that is likely to be the receptionist. He or she is often ignored by everyone. They're looked at as "gatekeepers," which means all they are is someone to get past. Believe me, they feel it too. Don't forget, everyone is important, but the receptionist knows about more people than anyone else and often knows how to get in contact with anyone since he or she has to do that for the president.

Here's what I did: I immediately contacted the president of the chamber and introduced myself. I emailed, left a phone message, and made sure to go to the first event I could where I knew she would be in attendance. Then I went right up and introduced myself face-to-face.

Here's what not to do: Everything I did in the paragraph above. It's just too presumptuous to think you'll matter to the president of the organization just because you paid a couple of hundred bucks to be there. And it's rude.

Here's what to do: Really meet the staff. Go ahead, introduce yourself to everyone on staff at the chamber, including the president. But when you do, make the meeting more about what you can do for them and less about what they can do for you. These people work very hard for very little pay. But they love the recognition and access the business provides them with. So a little attention will go a long way!

If you haven't already met everyone by attending an event, go by the chamber office and meet them. Actually, even if you've met them already, stop by the office and see what they do in their own environment. You don't need an appointment, but you do need to realize everyone might not be there at your beck and call. You might need to make a couple of trips to the chamber to meet everyone in their surroundings. And you might need to make an appointment to meet the president or vice president.

Now, once you've really met the chamber staff, chances are they'll ask you what you do and how they can help you. Many chamber staff members are careful not to sound like they can send you referrals because they're trying not to set the bar too high. But when they know you and know you know them, they'll be likely to think of you when the opportunity comes along where someone needs a solution that you can provide.

And just like earlier, they'll want to help if they can. So your Statement of Value, Ideal Customer Identity, and your Ideal Customer Association List will be invaluable when explaining to the staff just what you do, how you do it like no one else, and who will best benefit from knowing you.

Don't expect them to understand the first time around. But the more they see you and hear you talk about what you do—and the more you show genuine interest in them—the more likely it will be that you'll start to hear people say, "Someone from the chamber office sent me." Believe me, you'll love hearing that!

CHAPTER 11
Check the Calendar

Every chamber has a calendar you can check to find out what is scheduled for at least the next month. Most have this calendar online, and many even send a weekly email with upcoming events listed and links to RSVP to.

Don't delay in finding out what is going on and ensuring you are receiving emails from the chamber. While a chamber schedule is usually set in advance, many times an opportunity will arise that will not be on the calendar but will provide great value.

Here's one example from my experience. Laura Stack is a nationally known expert on productivity. She was in town to promote her new book, and her staff contacted me at the Metro Atlanta Chamber, asking if I'd promote her appearance at a nearby bookstore.

I was fortunate that I had become familiar with Laura and her work years earlier, and I knew her information would be valuable to my members. I didn't need to waste time doing research to see if this would be a good investment of resources for the chamber and its members.

As a side note, this is one of the biggest values of meeting people at the chamber. The people you meet will have such varied experiences from yours. You'll be exposed to ideas and opportunities that never come about in everyday life. More on that later.

Not only did I promote that appearance, but I also scheduled an appearance at our chamber and sent out a blast to the membership to build attendance. I had heard of Laura earlier in my career and loved her content, so I knew it was a can't-miss opportunity for our members.

Laura Stack (http://theproductivitypro.com/) taught me so much. Just one example was to use different colored folders to identify different projects or jobs. It made so much sense. Once something gets into a folder, it's hard to know what's in there and harder still to find what you're looking for quickly, especially if you are like me and have a tendency to not file things right away! To this day, my red folder holds the most important information I have and need quickly.

The only way I had to communicate this opportunity to our members was through email. Those members whose email addresses weren't accurate or up to date missed out.

As it turned out, we packed the house, and everyone appreciated the added value of an unexpected event.

Here's what I learned: The chamber calendar is fluid and often changes. It's important to know what's been added but just as important to know what might have been canceled. If preregistration is low, chambers will cancel an event. If you don't check the calendar, you might show up to an event that isn't happening. That's a big waste of time.

Here's what I did: It's twofold. First, I checked and rechecked my email address the chamber had and what lists they had me on. I even made sure I was on the Women's Business Network and Young Professionals email lists because they might have an opportunity that I would want to know about for some of my contacts, like my wife and kids.

Then I monitored my email (and I still do) to make sure I didn't fall off the list. Electronic systems fail, and I want to be certain I'm in the know with regard to chamber opportunities.

Next, I checked (and still do) the chamber calendar every Sunday night to ensure I have on my calendar all the events I want to attend, with reminders one day before. I RSVP for the events I know I will attend. I never RSVP unless I'm committed. And if for some reason I find I cannot attend, I contact the chamber and let them know with apologies for the short notice. It's just respectful.

Here's what to do: Contact the chamber and ask how to log in to your account. Most chambers now have systems that allow members to control their information and the email and communications lists themselves. If your chamber does not allow you to do it electronically, check with the staff to ensure you're on the lists of communications that matter to you.

In either case, ask what other emails and communications go out that you might not be thinking of. Many chambers will have governmental affairs, volunteer, community news, and other targeted lists you'll want to be a part of.

Finally, determine a time that works for you and set a reminder in your calendar to check the chamber calendar and update yours for the coming week. You've invested your money. Don't let something like poor planning get in the way of success in your membership. Be sure to RSVP for the events you want to attend, because there's something about committing to others that makes us follow through. Then attend with a plan.

A plan? That's right, you need a plan for every event you attend. This is the only way you'll maximize the value of your membership and ensure you're not just falling into the social aspect of chamber life.

And there's a big social aspect, not that it's bad. In fact, it's a necessary part in order to be top of mind with the people you meet. So going just to socialize and meet new people is one of the things you can put in your plan.

It's not as hard as it might sound, and the plan for each event will come more easily with the development of your Networking Plan (more on that later). For now, here are some considerations.

Sample Networking Plan Chart

Type of Event	Meet People Schedule Follow up	Learn Skills/ Get New Ideas	Exposure/ Branding	Enhance Standing
Training/ Education	Secondary	Primary		
Social/Mixer	Primary		Secondary	
Committee		Secondary		Primary
Community			Primary	Secondary

This is just an example of types of events and the benefits you might seek from attending them. It's vitally important to do this before you commit to attending because you just might find that an event you were thinking of attending doesn't provide you with enough benefit.

I mentioned that attending for the social aspect is a big part of it, and it is. But I never plan to just socialize. That's a waste of business time, and it sends the wrong message to everyone I meet. I want people to enjoy being around me, and I want people to socialize with me, but I never want to send the message that I'm simply "hanging out."

POWER TIP: When you meet someone at an event who is just "hanging out," you'll need an exit strategy. Stick out your hand to shake hands, look them straight in the eyes, and say, "It was nice meeting (or talking with) you." Then simply walk away. Everyone knows that means the conversation is over. Don't say something that builds expectations, such as "I'll be back" or "I hope to talk with you again." And never say, "I need to go to the bathroom" or "I need to talk to (someone else)."

Here's what I learned: Almost no one attends with a plan, and knowing that is a big advantage. People without a plan aren't usually successful, and they have a tendency to pull others in. When I finally started planning my results in advance, I found every event more beneficial. And when I did attend an event that wasn't giving me the results I wanted, I simply left. Yes, you can do that!

Here's what I did: Before RSVPing for an event, I would give good thought to what I hoped to accomplish. Then I'd ask myself, "Is it likely I can get that by attending? Is this the best use of my time right now?" Sometimes, I'd decide I wouldn't go. But when I did commit, I found success more often than not.

POWER TIP: Some chambers have the list of people who have RSVP'd online. It's a good idea to attend if you see that someone you need to meet is planning on attending. My wife met a key contact at a chamber luncheon, resulting in over $150,000 in business every year for five years (totaling over $1 million so far).

Here's what to do: Don't get too caught up in planning because in the beginning, you'll likely be looking for reasons not to attend. That's because you're uncomfortable and a bit scared of the new environment. Pick a small result you're seeking (e.g., Meet One New Person and Schedule a Follow Up). Then RSVP and go!

I strongly suggest you attend one of everything in the

beginning. If you can go, you should go. This is the best way to find out what is offered, who attends, and what you might offer and get from attending.

Just commit to attending everything once. Even if that means you have to go to something six months down the road, you might find a diamond in the rough in an event you previously thought you couldn't commit to. You might find that the prior engagement you thought you couldn't miss out on isn't so important now that you know the new one is better for you and your business.

CHAPTER 12

Attend Regularly: The What, When, and How

So, you've joined the chamber and you've started to get involved. You're keeping up with the calendar. That's great.

I know what you're thinking. "How much do I have to do to get the value?" This is the chapter where most people will quit. It's the nonsexy, repetitive part of chamber membership that can become monotonous and boring. But hang in there. This is where the money is, believe it or not!

In the prior section, I suggested you attend every event at least once. But in some chambers, that's nearly impossible. Some chambers have such a robust calendar that even the most committed members find it daunting. After all, there is work to do.

So, what does "attend regularly" mean?

Once you've found the events and meetings that bring you value, you can begin eliminating the ones that do not. Essentially, you'll be seeking the opportunities that give you the best chance to find fulfillment, meet the people you wish to meet, and where you can give the most to the group as well.

Here's what I learned: Knowing who might be attending what and when gives you quick access to the right people in the right environment. It's a quick path to success provided you know the rules.

In my experience, I've found the following people attend the following types of events and meetings:

Morning Meetings and Events: In general, the busiest, most successful people in the community will attend in the morning. CEOs of bigger companies, government officials, and harder-to-reach community leaders start their days early. You should too.

Here's what to do: Arrive early. Choose a seat up front and spend time as a greeter at the entrance. This gives you the best opportunity to meet someone you're hoping to meet.

Luncheons and Midday Meetings: In general, people who attend lunchtime meetings are usually middle management and sales people. These are people who don't always have control over their calendars and therefore have to meet new people on their own time. But if they can attend a chamber event and have lunch too, their lunch is often paid for by the company they work for, or they can write off the expense. This is the best place to meet potential networking partners because these folks meet a lot of people.

Here's what to do: Arrive early. Choose a seat that is on the end of a table near the host stand. Be prepared to give your self-introduction (more on that later) first in case it happens that way. Again, spend time greeting attendees.

After Hours and Evening Events: This is a mixed bag because the types of events held in the evening vary wildly. After hours (mixers or cocktail receptions) attract everyone, but they are difficult avenues for really connecting with people you don't know. This is because everyone is "winding down" from the day. But if you know how to meet people in these settings, you'll walk away with valuable contacts (more on that later). Evening events are often reserved for the big chamber dinners (e.g., Annual Meetings), and virtually every type of chamber member attends these. Since the larger companies usually sponsor tables or the event itself, it is a prime opportunity to meet people from these companies.

Here's what to do: Arrive early (are you seeing a trend?). Seek out those who are alone or not meeting others. Ask questions. It is easy for people who are new or who don't know what to do to be overlooked or blend into the walls at After Hours and Mixers. Do your best to introduce someone who is having trouble meeting people to someone else. Seek to have 3-5 quality conversations.

Here's what not to do: Don't overindulge in food or drink. It's easy to be judged at these events, and rarely does one who spends all his time at the buffet or the bar get judged favorably.

Ribbon Cuttings: These are a staple of chambers. New businesses and new members are often offered a ribbon cutting as a way to get them to join and get involved in the chamber. Don't be fooled by the size of a ribbon cutting. A smaller event is often better for you since the host will appreciate your attendance, and you'll be able to spend more one-on-one time with people.

Here's what to do: A nice touch is to bring a small gift because most people won't. Another way to stand out is to send a card of congratulations prior to the ribbon cutting. When you arrive, you'll already be someone the host is excited to meet.

Committee Meetings (including volunteer meetings). This is a fantastic opportunity for you. People who work together side by side on something of importance can't help but build a bond. You can find virtually anyone you need to at a committee or volunteer meeting if you know their interests.

> **Here's what to do:** Find a committee that you can embrace and attend. Get involved. Donate your time and expertise. It bears repeating: amazing things happen when you work side by side with people on a common goal or mission. And when you truly care about what you are doing, it shows—and shows you in the best possible light.

> **Here's what not to do:** Don't fake it. If you can't embrace what the group is all about, everyone will be able to tell. And everyone will tell their friends you are fake. Just don't.

Training and Educational Programs: Every chamber has a schedule of training programs they offer to improve business in their community. Sometimes the chamber will partner with a local college or other institution. Sometimes, like my example with Laura Stack earlier, they'll partner with a publicist or media outlet, and often, they'll simply promote an event on their own. Usually, who attends has more to do with the speaker than anything else. High-profile business leaders, authors, politicians, and media "stars" will attract a larger, more diverse crowd. Specialized training speakers and coaches will attract a specific crowd seeking specific knowledge.

Here's what I learned: World-class educational opportunities will be available to you through your local chamber of commerce, but the quality of programming will be dependent upon the reach of your chamber. If your chamber can't put 100 people in a room, it's unlikely you'll have a senator, governor, New York Times Best Selling Author, or another high-profile speaker at your chamber. That doesn't exclude quality programming from your reach, it just may be well disguised with a lesser-known presenter.

This can be an advantage, though, if you are seeking training specific to your needs because you can have more one-on-one time with the trainer.

I was a presenter at the American Chamber of Commerce Executives Annual Conference in Pittsburgh, Pennsylvania, in 2008. I followed a lot of my own advice. I checked the calendar, determined which events and programs I wanted to attend, and yes, I got there early.

Here's what I learned: CEOs of organizations get started early. They often arrive early to events and programs they will attend. I learned this in a very powerful, wonderful way.

Steve Forbes, chief executive of Forbes and former candidate for president of the United States, was scheduled to speak early one morning. I got there one hour early. I walked in the room, and to my surprise, there was one person sitting alone at a table up front. It was Steve Forbes.

I spent the next 45 minutes alone with him. We talked about politics, publishing, and any number of other topics. I'll never forget that somehow the topic of "giving back" came up. To paraphrase him, "I hate that term. It sounds like I took something that wasn't mine. I'm happy to give, but giving back just doesn't sound right to me." It was an amazing day.

Here's what to do: Arrive early. (Yes, I know I've already made this point.)

Once you've attended one of everything and narrowed it down to the events, meetings, and programs you know you want to attend more often, now you have to make time to commit fully to them.

The real power in chamber membership is the familiarity and association you have with people you see there. But you are about to enter the danger zone.

Too often, people become so focused on results they fail

to realize they are getting them, just not in the way they expect, so they don't see the progress.

I can't begin to tell you how many people I've talked with who dropped out of or quit going to the chamber. The vast majority of people who quit do so too soon. And of those, the most frequent reason they quit is, "I just saw the same people over and over." What a shame.

What these people fail to realize, and what I hope you will, is that this is when the good stuff starts. If you are in the room with the right people, either prospects or prospective networking partners, you can't help but win if you continue to be there.

And it's a great investment of your time and resources. Let's say you run an ad for your product or service in the local newspaper, in a magazine, or online through social media. First, you'll need to know exactly what to say, how to say it, and whom to say it to in order to get a return. And even when you do, you'll still have to be face-to-face with them (even if that is virtually) to go from interested prospect to active customer. In this case, you invest money and time.

And you do at the chamber too. But here's the difference: At the chamber, you get instant feedback as to what works and what doesn't. It's easier to narrow your prospect target, and you can avoid (mostly) your message falling on a poor prospect who will take hours of your time and effort. And best of all, if you do see someone over and over who begins to like you but doesn't need your product or service, he or she will be more likely to pass on your name with an endorsement to someone who does. Try to get a Facebook ad to do that!

Here's what I learned: The more often you see someone, the more likely you are to know about them. And the more we know about people or things, the more likely we are to like them. Chambers are a perfect place to see people on a regular basis, and you can't help but become known in that environment. Being known leads to being liked, and being liked leads to being trusted. Being trusted leads to business.

You will shorten the time and effort to being trusted by being a regular attendee with other regular attendees. Being there on a regular basis shows you are reliable. People love doing business with reliable people.

Here's what I did: I kept going to the same events over and over. And you know what happened? I became known, liked, and trusted by many of the attendees. Better still, because I went all the time, I noticed there was at least 50 percent turnover in attendees. Simply put, that theory that you see the same people over and over holds true only if you quit going.

Here's what to do: I encouraged you to narrow down the events first because you'll need to genuinely enjoy what you attend to get past the initial phase of slow results combined with familiar faces. But stick with it. Keep going. There's gold (results) in those people you're connecting with.

CHAPTER 13

Ask Questions

I've already covered it to some extent, but in this section, we'll drill down to the core of the how-to, why-to, and what-to of asking questions.

Being a great conversationalist is often just being skillful at asking questions and listening to the answers. People like to talk about themselves, and when you show an interest in others, they will naturally think you are interesting too.

As you meet people at events and programs of the chamber, ask them questions about their business. Some simple questions that always get people talking include:
- What do you do?
- How long have you been doing it?
- What got you started in that line of work?
- How long have you been in the area?
- Who would be a good referral for you?

You may not get a chance to ask one of the questions you'll want to ask. "Do you have a card?" That's because many people will offer a card to you before you ask for it.

Here's what I learned: Offering a business card before someone asks for it often has a negative effect. You'll appear pushy, self-centered, and salesy if you offer your card first. In addition, from my surveying of people who attend events, over 90 percent of all cards that are given unsolicited end up in a trash can. Don't waste their time or your money.

Here's what I did: I always ask for a card just after I find out what kind of work someone does, unless I know from the line of work they are in that I cannot help them nor can they help me. I ask right after they tell me their line of work because that's the most likely time they'll be offering one and the time where I'll need to refresh my brain with their name. It also puts me in a position to jot a note or two on the back of the card and the ability to end the conversation quickly and graciously if I need to.

Here's what to do: Ask for a card from the people you meet just after they tell you what company they work for or the work they do. Look down at it, see their name, look them in the eye, and say, "Thanks, Bob."

Here's what not to do: I used to say never offer your card unless asked for it, but I've changed that slightly. There are times when you'll meet someone who clearly wants your card but fails to ask for it. Of course, you should ask for theirs. If you hear statements similar to, "I'd really like to call you tomorrow" or "I'll be in touch this week," make it easier for them by providing a card. You can even jot a note on the back that reminds them of the action they wanted to take. Don't get too excited. Rarely does anyone call when they say they will, and if they do, it's almost always to sell you something.

POWER TIP: Keep your business cards in your right pocket (that means always choose to wear something that has a right pocket—ladies too!). This way, when you shake hands with your right hand, it is occupied but your left is available to take their card. Place the cards you receive in your left pocket and keep your cards in your right. This eliminates getting your card mixed up with someone else's or, worse yet, giving a card you just received to the person you meet next.

When you get the answers, jot some notes on the back of their business card. This will give you the ability to remember who you met and what is important to them.

You'll meet a lot of people at events. Knowing about

them will help you decide if they are a good fit for you. Remember, while you are always asking questions to get people talking and have them find you more interesting because you're a great listener, you're also asking questions to prequalify the people you meet to become a part of your network.

It's like an interview. In the end, you have to decide if you'll extend an invitation to become a part of your network. This requires serious consideration. Do not take this lightly. That's why I recommend you decide in advance who you want to meet. This way, you don't find yourself picking up a new referral or networking partner who isn't a good fit just because you were looking for someone to talk to.

We often overlook asking questions of the staff, volunteer committee chairs, and the board of directors.

Now that you're getting plugged in, it's time you dug a bit deeper to find out what's really going on in and through the chamber. If you asked questions of these folks in the beginning, you would have most certainly heard the talking points of the chamber. These are the words and phrases the chamber staff uses most and that are heard most by the volunteers and board. So it's only natural that these are the words you'll hear in the beginning because they require no thought to recite.

But when you are clearly interested and involved, and when you've demonstrated that you can be trusted, you'll find you get to the marrow of the matter rather quickly. You'll find out how the members really feel about the chamber and, most importantly, why.

This can be powerful for you if you ask questions that lead to uncovering problems you might be able to solve within the chamber. A couple of good examples are:

1. You notice a staff member is always setting up and tearing down after events and that she has little or no help. Asking if this is the norm and if she'd like to have help will obviously solicit yes answers. But asking, "Isn't someone scheduled to help you?" might solicit valuable information about how she feels about her job. Then, when you offer to help, you're solving her problem. That's making a friend, and it's what you would have done already. It's just positioned a bit differently.

2. You see that a volunteer committee chair is often doing most of the work of the committee. Asking, "Can you tell me a bit more about the work your committee does?" will lead to an explanation. Then asking, "I know what you guys are doing is important. How can I help?" will lead to an invitation to join. Joining gives you a position of importance on the committee and in the chamber.

3. You really don't know what you might like to do within the chamber, but you know you should get involved. Asking a key staff member about committee work often ends in an invitation to join the committee they need the most help with. But this isn't always your best fit. Asking a board member to explain the different opportunities often gives you a better understanding and opportunity to get involved where you are best suited. And you might even get an invitation to a board meeting to meet everyone and have them explain the different committees.

It's important to ask a lot of questions. It's really the only way to learn what you need to know to get and give the most.

CHAPTER 14:

Create a Networking Plan

Everyone is networking every day. Most people don't like to network and claim they don't, but then they recommend a restaurant or movie, ask directions of a local, or simply strike up a conversation in the checkout line, and voila, they are networking.

Ask virtually any local business and they'll tell you they get most of their business from word of mouth or referral. Isn't that networking? Networking gets a very bad rap. And when you attend a few chamber events and have Johnny Shotgun unload his card on you unsolicited, when someone verbally vomits their spiel on you, and when you walk away having been invited to three opportunity meetings for products you know nothing about, well, it's understandable why people hate networking.

Yet everyone knows networking works. And in all my

years of working with tens of thousands of business people and chamber members, I can tell you I've met fewer than ten people who had a networking plan.

A follow-up plan? A sales plan? A meeting-people plan? Sure, but a networking plan? Hardly ever.

And here's why. No plan survives contact with someone else. Networking is all about contact with multiple people multiple times. So, a networking plan is something of a misnomer.

Misnomer or not, it's the best term to use in this situation, and in truth, what you've done so far has begun your networking plan. Everything good that will happen in your chamber experience will hinge on what you do now.

Will you complete the plan or stop right here? The reason I ask is because so many people will stop right here. After all, you've done a lot already. You've invested a lot of money, effort, and time. And you have likely begun to get some results.

This is where most chamber members stop. Stopping now will ensure you'll never find the success you hoped to in joining the chamber or buying this book. But I promise, just like investing over the long term, continuing to invest in the chamber experience will pay exponential benefits because of the investments you've made so far.

These are the essential components of a Networking Plan:

- Who do you need to meet?
- Who can you help?
- Who is missing in your current network?
- What events are likely to attract the people you need to meet and those missing in your network?
- What will be your self-introduction that attracts the right people to be interested in you?
- What interests do you have that your target audience has?
- How many people should you meet at each event?
- How many people do you need to meet to get to one you will add to your network?
- How many people do you need to meet to get to one sale?
- How many people do you need to help to get one who will help you?
- How many one-on-one meetings do you need to have to narrow these down?

A networking plan is actually a plan to build relationships. And while everything you have done and will do leads to building relationships, the fastest way is to have one-on-one meetings. If you need more help building your networking plan, visit MillionDollarMeetings.com.

CHAPTER 15

Have one-on-ones

Once you begin meeting people at the chamber and events, you'll need to find out more about them to determine if they fit your network. And you'll want them to know more about you.

A one-on-one meeting is the perfect forum for this. You've met someone (likely several people) who you think might be a good fit for you. Sometimes they'll be a good fit for your network, sometimes they'll be a good referral partner, sometimes they're a prospect for business for you, and sometimes they're a prospect as a vendor. In any case, you need to get to know them better.

Don't make the mistake of asking for a lunch meeting at this stage. That's far too big a commitment, and when having lunch, each party feels obligated to make it work.

Here's what I learned: Too often, we overcommit when meeting new people. It takes many forms.

We say, "I hope to see you again" as a way to end a conversation, and the other person thinks we really mean it. We say, "Call me" when we really hope they don't. Or we say, "Let's have lunch" when all we really should say is "Let's have coffee" when we want to know more about someone. Overcommitting is one of the biggest reasons people find chamber life and networking unattractive.

Here's what I did: My friend and business partner Ben Turpin taught me to simply say, "Meet me at Starbucks. I'd like to learn more about you and what you do." Notice I didn't say anything that sounds like I'm making a promise. I used to say, "I'd like to see if we can work together" or "I'd like to see how I can help you," thinking I was making the meeting more attractive. But if I need to make the meeting more attractive, do I really need to be meeting at all? Not really.

Here's what to do: Start inviting people to meet you at Starbucks or your favorite coffee house. Most people realize a meeting for coffee is going to be short, and most everyone has a few minutes to spare in hopes it will be the beginning of a new relationship. If you want to know more about how to make these meetings more productive, check out our book *Meet Me At Starbucks* (available on Amazon).

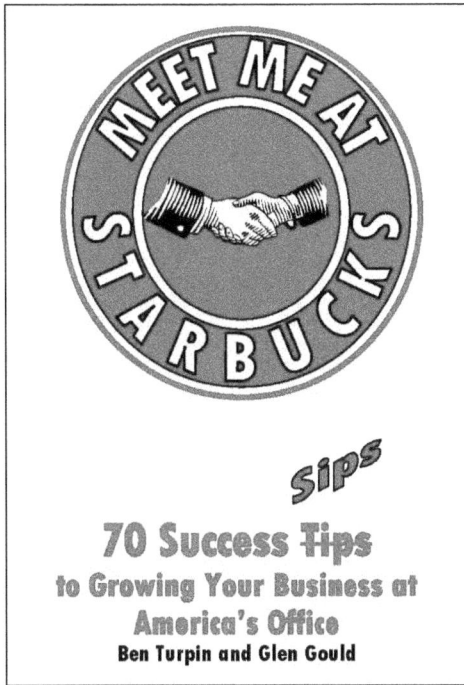

Meet Me At Starbucks Book Cover

The coffee meeting needs to be informal. It's conversational. But it's also with a purpose. While your objective is to further understand what makes your meeting partner tick, what it is that she is looking for, and how the two of you might connect better, the real purpose is to refine the preliminary choices you've made to be prepared to give the first referral.

CHAPTER 16

Give the first referral

You've invited someone, or several people, to meet you for coffee. Hopefully you've thought about what you're going to say and what you hope to accomplish in the meeting. After all, the whole idea of having a plan for who you need to meet probably uncovered what you hope to accomplish by meeting them. But if it didn't, decide now before the meeting how you hope this meeting will turn out.

We get what we want and need most often by giving others what they want and need. It's a simple rule that we all too often violate. Just remember, the person you are meeting with has hopes and expectations too. What do you think he or she would like to get from the meeting?

Since this is a business book, and since we're talking about business, chances are the person you are going to meet for coffee is interested in business. Chances are, he or she would like to find a way to add to his or her business by meeting you.

You now know what your meeting partner wants. They want more for themselves.

Here's what I learned: You can be assured that everyone is thinking about themselves first, last, and always. Even when someone does something charitable, it can be traced back to how it makes them feel about themselves. Never lose sight of the fact that they aren't interested in you, they're interested in how you can help them. I'm not being cynical here. It's just a fact. People think about themselves.

Chances are you already know something about them and their business. When you met them, did you ask them what they were looking for? Did you ask them the Million Dollar Question? Probably not since we haven't covered it yet.

It's called the Million Dollar Question because it can literally mean millions of dollars for you and the people you meet. I first heard it called the Million Dollar Question by Ben Turpin. Asking it or a version of it and acting on what you learn will reap great rewards for the people you meet. And it will endear you to people and connect them to you in ways you just might not imagine.

So here it is.

POWER TIP: Ask the Million Dollar Question after you've talked a bit. You've exchanged the basic questions discussed earlier, and now you're getting to the point where you're about to wrap up the conversation. Ideally, you'll ask this question before your one-on-one meeting. "As I go through my day, I meet a lot of people. Tell me, how will I know I've met someone you need to meet or a perfect referral for you?"

Be ready for a puzzled look and a stammering response. Most people never stop thinking about themselves long enough to ask someone what they want, so you'll be different immediately. Be ready to help them help you by further clarifying. "Who do you need to meet?" "Who is your ideal client?" "Tell me about your best customer."

Lead them to the answer, and then be sure to write it down in front of them. Jot it on a business card. If you don't have one and haven't asked for one, now is the time. Let them see you acting on the question right away. And be ready to answer the same question because they just might take your lead. (We'll cover that in detail in a following section, "How to introduce yourself").

Here's what I did: I always try to have in mind their answer to the Million Dollar Question. So, I would be taking notes the whole time I'm asking questions, being certain to narrow the search to a few key points. If they couldn't answer the question, I'd recap, saying, "Well, Bob, you said you work well with people who..." and you said that "people who live in town are good prospects too."

Like a good lawyer, you need to know the answer to the question you are asking, or at least have a few key features of the person they are describing to ensure you don't make them uncomfortable and, therefore, uncomfortable around you.

Here's what to do: Practice is the only way to get good at this. After each meeting, try to recap what was said to you. After you jot the notes on the back of the cards, look back and recap with the person you met. "Bob, I just want to go back over this one more time. You're looking for people who live in town who...." It works. And best of all, it shows you really care. Now you better make sure to follow up and follow through (covered next).

Based on what you learned in your first meeting, and on their answer to the Million Dollar Question, you have searched your network and contact list and come up with a couple of people who you think might be good connections or referrals for them. But do not give these out just yet.

Throughout the meeting, you are simply refining the preliminary choices you made to find the best possible referral you can give. And now you're ready to give the first referral.

In giving the first referral, you should position it by saying, "Based on what you've told me, I think Mary Jones would be a good referral for you. She would be a wonderful resource for you, and I think both of you are serving the same market segment for different services. If you'd like, I can call Mary and introduce you."

POWER TIP: If you've done a good job of prequalifying your new networking partner, and if you have a strong relationship with Mary Jones, you should have called Mary in advance to let her know you might be calling with a connection for her. The best first referrals will be referrals to networking partners, not to people your new connection can sell to. In this way, you can see if your new connection will follow through properly before you endorse them to provide service to someone else.

As you grow your network, you'll become known as a connector of people. This means you'll know a lot of people, a lot of people will know you, and you'll get to meet more people still. And giving the first referral gets the relationship going. It shows you are interested in their success, and we already know that people won't care about us until they know we care about them. Giving the first referral demonstrates you care.

CHAPTER 17

Follow up and follow through

A critical point has been reached. You've done a lot to get to meet some people and have them meet you. Not only are you meeting people, but you're also meeting the right people since you've worked your networking plan. It will all be lost if you don't follow up and follow through.

Here's what I did: I began using the Million Dollar Question at every event. Whenever I met someone new, I'd go through the normal questions and then would ask the Million Dollar Question. I clarified, jotted a note on the back of a card, and then my mind went to work. If I met someone that night who might fit, I'd introduce them. If not, I'd go back to my home or office and begin searching my database for a connection. And I did it right away.

POWER TIP: Part of your networking plan needs to

be setting time aside after each meeting to review the connections you made and decide if they will get a coffee invite or just a follow-up card or email. Every connection gets one or more of the following:

- An email saying, "It was nice meeting you." This person gets no further follow-up.

- A card or note saying, "It was great meeting you." This is for people you know you will connect with further.

- A phone call. "It was nice meeting you. Would you like to get a cup of coffee?"

Here's what to do: Begin marking your calendar now for time after each event to follow up using one of the three techniques above. Whenever you book time for an event, a one-on-one, or a meeting of any type, add a time in your calendar immediately following to follow up.

I've known a few professionals who carry thank-you cards and postcards in their car. When they go back to the car after a meeting or event, they quickly jot a simple note to the person or persons they've met. It's a powerful way to stay on top of your follow-up. Just be sure to add them to your follow-up sequence or your CRM (Client or Customer Relationship Management) system.

Or you can simply find an article or story that might be interesting to the person you recently met and send it to her. Add a personal note saying, "Saw this and thought of you."

And there's absolutely no reason not to follow up today. There are so many easy-to-use programs available to automate the follow-up process. Whether you use a Day-timer, electronic calendar, or a proprietary customer relationship manager, it's easier than ever to follow up and follow through.

My friend Michael Moore, a former banker, taught me how to follow up. I'm sure he has a system just like I do, but he does it in such a way you'd never know it. I guess what I'm saying is that he makes you feel like you're important to him, regardless of what you can do for him or what he can do for you. Fact is, it isn't an act with Michael. It's genuine and something we all should endeavor to do.

Since Michael has a system he follows, he never fails to connect people with problems to people with solutions. And because he does so, he keeps contact with an extraordinary number of people. He has access to high-level executives, members of government, and world-class authors like me (OK, that's a bit boastful).

When you keep in touch with people as well as Michael does, you cannot help but be well known and invited to a lot of functions. This is one of the most powerful things about chamber membership as well.

> **POWER TIP:** Following up well gets noticed, and doing so will ensure you have access to a lot of people. The chamber gives you access to a very diverse group. You'll meet people who have ideas and opinions much different than your own. This is one of the best things that can happen to you. You'll find answers to problems you have through people you'd never have met if you weren't at the chamber. People who have experiences you've never had often have answers you've never thought of.

Not long ago I met a woman at a chamber event who owns a liquor store. Our county is "dry," meaning that spirits are sold only by the drink at restaurants. You can buy beer and wine but not hard liquor. To do that, you have to go to the county line. And that's where her store is.

As we talked, she mentioned she'd like to be able to reach the new people moving into the county. As a side note, when I moved here, I drove up and down the main highway looking for a liquor store and was dumbfounded when I finally called a work colleague and learned we didn't have a liquor store.

That store owner's thought was that if she could reach people as they moved to the area, they would find out about her store first, and that would be the best way to grow her business. As it turns out, in our dry cleaning pickup and delivery business, one of our key strategies is mailing to new movers.

I told her how to get the list of new movers (NewHome-Data.net). It's surprisingly inexpensive, and it works well. So a dry cleaning service had a solution a liquor store owner needed. Had we not met at the chamber, she'd still be looking for that solution.

Oh, and just to show that it works both ways, I was able to get a wine my wife likes at a great price through their liquor store.

Follow up and follow through. It's where the relationships develop, the trust is solidified, and the money is made.

Here's what to do: Develop your own way to ensure you follow up. Plan follow-up time after each encounter to jot a note, email, or make a call to follow up. It can be as simple as setting aside thirty minutes each morning to follow up with people you connected with the day before.

I use InfusionSoft and recommend it highly. If you want something effective but inexpensive, I've used MailChimp with great results. I've also used my own system I learned in the car business with a simple notebook and tabs for days of the month and months of the year. There's no excuse: Create your system now.

Here's what not to do: Never, ever send a mass email to everyone you meet in a meeting. I can't tell you how many times I've received an email after going to a networking event that says:

Hi!

It was nice meeting you at the chamber event last night.

PDQ Company is the leader in blah, blah, blah and all about me paragraph after paragraph.

I hope to see you again soon,

Ed

OMG, I delete these emails quickly, and you probably do too. Unfortunately, you can never overcome a blatant, impersonal, blanket email once sent. It's called SPAM for a reason. No one likes it. Just don't do it.

CHAPTER 18

Volunteer and offer to help

While I've covered this to some degree earlier, it wasn't covered as a strategy to build your brand, reputation, and relationship with people at the chamber. You can offer to help and volunteer as soon as you join the chamber, but it isn't likely you'll get further than being a greeter.

But that's a good start. Offer to help as a greeter. The chamber needs people who will meet people at the door and welcome them, direct them to where they need to go, and make them feel at home.

You can also offer to help distribute information at tables, set up, tear down, and transport items to and from venues. You might call it grunt work, but that's exactly what most chamber people need help with but won't ask for.

When you demonstrate that you're willing to do the basics, and that you can be relied upon at any time, you'll soon be ready to take the next steps.

Understand this. The next two techniques are graduate school techniques. You cannot implement them until you've done the first eight.

Volunteering to participate on a committee is a big step. It requires commitment and the skill to contribute. But it can be the most rewarding thing you'll ever do, both in business and in your personal life.

Being on a committee will give you access to people you normally won't be in contact with and in a way that most people never experience.

Here's what I learned: Amazing things happen and long-term relationships are formed when you work side by side with people for a common cause. If you volunteer your time and work with others who do the same and have a common interest, you'll often bypass every other marketing opportunity and rise to the top of mind with those you worked with. What's more, you'll often forge lifelong friendships.

Here's what I did: My experience was somewhat accidental. But what I did was volunteer at the first opportunity I saw.

I was attending a meeting of the Punta Gorda Business Alliance, and someone at the lectern said, "If you're interested in serving on a committee, please let me know." He then went around the room with a hat asking for business cards. I dropped mine in. And that was that.

Until 18 months later. I received a call from one of the board members of the alliance saying, "Congratulations, Glen, you've been voted onto the board of the alliance." I was stunned. I didn't even remember volunteering. But after a while, it all came back to me.

While this story does have a strange beginning, it also has a powerful ending. Several months later, I was chosen as vice president. A couple of months later, our executive director informed me she had cancer and she wasn't going to win the battle.

Because I was now the vice president of the organization (now the Punta Gorda Chamber of Commerce), I was in a position to apply for and get the job of executive director. That was the beginning of my chamber career.

One day, I'm a local dry cleaner. The next, I'm receiving calls from the mayor, I'm meeting with members of Congress, and I'm hosting major public and business development events.

I'm not saying you'll become the head of your chamber

if you volunteer, but I can tell you if you volunteer and really apply yourself, your life will change for the better.

Here's what not to do: Don't be like me. Don't volunteer and then wait for someone to call.

Here's what to do: Learn all you can about the committees at the chamber and determine where your skills can best be used. Then meet with the committee chair and/or a staff member to discuss the opportunity to serve and why you feel you'd be a good fit for that committee. Demonstrate the skills and strengths you bring. In essence, sell yourself to the committee.

Most chambers have limited resources. They lack the money, infrastructure, and staff to really expand their offerings and create new programs that attract and retain members. That's why so much of the chamber experience becomes repetitive and mundane.

Chambers desperately need new members and ideas. And when they find energetic new members with ideas, that's when something amazing happens.

My friend Ben Turpin joined the Sarasota Chamber of Commerce and quickly found himself running the Power Networking Lunch. It was a weekly lunch meeting and networking opportunity that he and a few others made into the "must attend" event each week.

It was simple. You're going to have lunch, so why not make it a Power Networking Lunch? Get together with other business people in the area, enjoy lunch, learn about what they do, get to tell them what you do, and perhaps make a connection or two. It was brilliant.

Here's what I did: With my friend and business partner Ben Turpin, I volunteered to run the Power Networking Lunch for several chambers. In doing so, Ben and I met everyone, learned about everyone, and could connect everyone.

Here's what to do: Does your chamber have a regular, predictable lunch program? If so, join in and ask to help. Collect money, greet people at the door, or just help folks get acquainted. If not, launch one! Need help? Visit MillionDollarMeetings.com/PNL for ideas on starting and maintaining a Power Networking Lunch.

Lunch not your thing? Can't break away? I ran a breakfast meeting for a couple of years. Breakfast meetings can be very beneficial since many busy people can only break away for breakfast. The rules are about the same as for Power Networking Lunch except often breakfasts have themes and speakers.

Need help? Visit MillionDollarMeetings.com/ breakfast.

So you don't want the expense of a meal, but you really like the idea of hosting a networking group or predicable event. Here are a few ideas.

Leads to Business: This program is pure networking. Everyone gets a chance to speak, and everyone meets everyone. Each meeting, two of the regular attendees get a 5- to 10-minute mini-presentation to help everyone become more familiar with them and their business. But here's the real twist: Everyone gets a lead or referral every time. Want to know more? Visit MillionDollarMeetings.com/Leads.

Leads to Answers: This is a smaller program with exclusivity in the group. Only one attendee from a business category can attend. It is by invitation only, so you can pick who you associate with. This group becomes each other's advisory board. Exchange ideas, get answers to problems, and network. Everyone wins. Learn more at MillionDollar-Meetings.com/Answers.

Small Business Committee or Awards: Many chambers suffer from an identity crisis. Since so many bigger companies have the available money to donate and sponsor events, they seem to get all the recognition. Small business often feels ignored. If your chamber doesn't have a Small Business Committee or Awards Program, consider launching one. Learn more at MillionDollarMeetings.com/Small-Business.

The opportunities to launch meaningful, impactful, and lasting programs are limited only by your imagination. Many of the programs I've launched are still running years and even decades later.

You can leave your mark and make a lasting impression by launching something meaningful in your chamber.

CHAPTER 19

Take a leadership role

This really goes part and parcel with volunteering. Nearly all leadership roles within the chamber are voluntary. Unless you work for a company that has deep pockets, the only real way to land a leadership role is to work your way up.

Sure, I found myself on the board before I did any volunteer work, but that was a most unusual occurrence. My board service began on the board of the Punta Gorda Business Alliance. We were a small group of businesspeople who had banded together to represent the interests of Punta Gorda first, and then the greater community of Charlotte County.

The only real chamber in town, the Charlotte County Chamber of Commerce, had two locations, one in Punta Gorda that operated largely as a visitors' center and one in Port Charlotte, the main office, close to county government.

Each organization existed in harmony until August 2004.

August 13, 2004, Hurricane Charley made landfall in Punta Gorda, Florida. A major hurricane had not hit the west coast of Florida in 40 years. Punta Gorda was "old" Florida. Old structures, old planning, old people. Our city was not prepared.

Nor was our business community. Punta Gorda was the only incorporated city and the county seat of Charlotte County. Like so many other counties, Charlotte County spans 858 square miles and includes a dozen or so communities, all unincorporated.

It would seem that Punta Gorda would be the hub of business, and while many government functions and business activities did happen in town, much of the county government business happened and happens "across the river" in Port Charlotte.

In the wake of Hurricane Charley, governmental and other agencies poured into our community to provide aid, security, and restore essential services. When they did, they came looking for organizations they could leverage to get the word out. They came looking for the Chamber of Commerce.

Punta Gorda didn't have a chamber. We had a business

alliance. Relief agencies don't look for business alliances.

These agencies found what they were looking for in the Charlotte County Chamber of Commerce. When they did, any needs specific to Punta Gorda became secondary to the needs of the greater community. Perhaps it should have been that way all along, but devoid of a chamber, Punta Gorda never had a say.

So once the debris was removed and roads cleared, once we began to get back to as normal a life as we could, our business alliance voted to become a chamber of commerce. It was a very controversial decision.

We had a few members on our board who were also on the board of the Charlotte County Chamber of Commerce. This created strife, broke friendships, and created a sense of betrayal.

A pretty close friend and ardent advocate for me (we'll call him Bill because that was his name) became a vocal antagonist of our chamber and me. It was a strained relationship that never healed.

I tell this story for two reasons. First, it shows how unusual it was for me to become a board member before any volunteer work was done, and second, as a warning to you if you choose to take a leadership role.

Being a leader means making tough choices. It means you will choose an unpopular route sometimes because you believe the results will be better for your organization even though you might lose a friend or two in the process. It requires commitment.

Boards are often made up of heads of committees, subcommittees, and the executive committee, the titled members such as Chair, President, Vice Chair or President, Chair or President Elect, Secretary, Treasurer, etc.

Here's what I did: Once I was on the board and once I saw an opportunity to lead the leaders (become an executive committee member), I let everyone know I wanted it. I explained that I felt I could bring new ideas and even shared some of them at the risk of having them adopted by others without having me on board. It didn't matter. I wanted the organization to move forward, and I knew if my ideas were a part of it, eventually I would be too.

Here's what to do: After you've volunteered, served on a committee, and really come to understand the chamber and its mission, interview a few board members and find out if service has been rewarding for them and would be rewarding for you. Ask the tough questions, and don't be afraid to mention you're interested in board service. And have a vision for what you can bring to the organization.

Here's what not to do: Don't do it just for yourself. Of course, people will tell you that you should be unselfish and do everything out of benevolence for the organization. What hogwash. You will do your best for the organization when you remember it is the organization first, then you. But don't kid yourself, there's a personal reason you'll volunteer to lead. It might be recognition, or respect, or even some return on investment of your time, but we all serve to serve ourselves too.

The biggest change in your business and your life will come when you stretch and grow through doing things you haven't done before. Serving on a committee or board will give you experience in so many things you just can't get anywhere else.

You'll learn about working with people you may not like or agree with. You'll learn about finance, marketing, human resources, and business development. You'll learn Roberts Rules of Order, and you'll learn how not to do a lot of things too. It's amazingly beneficial.

You just might learn about public relations in the same way I did. Shortly after I became president of the Punta Gorda Chamber of Commerce, I was visited by a local journalist. He said he was doing a story on me, so of course I was excited to be interviewed.

Steve was, well, a stereotypical journalist born of the hippie generation. Although he was in his sixties, he had long gray hair pulled back into a full ponytail, and it was tucked up into his Tilly hat. He had round, wire-rimmed glasses. He wore jeans and a corduroy jacket (in Florida in July, no less) with a plaid shirt and woven tie. And he wore Birkenstocks.

He carried a small spiral-bound notepad and took notes with a pencil. Steve was very good at his job, and he loved it.

He entered my office, and we shook hands. I motioned for him to sit in one of the two chairs across from my desk. I asked if he wanted water or coffee, and he took the coffee. Then, the interview began.

At first, it was all fun and games. He asked the easy stuff. Where I was from, what brought me to Punta Gorda, what I did before I was the chamber president. It was easy.

And then, just as naturally as it had been so far, it all turned very foreign. Steve asked me a question about my friend Bill who'd become a vocal antagonist of our chamber and had resigned from the board. I'll never forget my response or what happened next.

"Bill? That blowhard? He doesn't know what he's talking about," I said.

Steve gently placed his notepad down on my desk. The pencil was placed on top of it. He looked down and removed his glasses and hat, and when he did, his ponytail fell out. He put the glasses and hat on the desk next to his notepad and pencil.

He slowly and deliberately rose from his chair, stepped to the left, and sat in the adjacent chair. With a deep breath, he looked up at me, his eyes riveted on mine. And then he did the greatest favor perhaps anyone has ever done for me.

With his finger pointed up in the air, making the number 1, he said, "I will give you one. You get one time to say something you wish you hadn't that I won't publish. This is that one. Remember, whatever you say, I will use it, and I'll likely use something dumb you say to your detriment."

And then, just as slowly and deliberately as he had risen from the previous chair, he returned to it. He tucked his hair in his hat, put on his glasses, picked up his notepad and pencil, and said, "Now I don't believe you've answered my question."

To which I replied, "My esteemed colleague is mistaken." And that was the quote that was printed.

Here's what to do: Remember, you may be asked to give a quote on behalf of the chamber. Be sure you understand the chamber policy and that you are one of the ones authorized to speak to the press. Then, by all means, remember what Steve told me: The press will use whatever you say and often to your detriment.

It's worth repeating. You'll learn so much more than you ever thought possible when you get involved and serve on a chamber board. And in the process, you'll become known in the chamber and community as a leader. And people like to do business with and hang out with leaders.

CHAPTER 20

How to introduce yourself

Even if you never attend a single chamber meeting, you need to know how to introduce yourself when you meet people at the grocery store, at church, or at a business meeting. If you're in business, at some point when you meet someone new, you'll talk about business.

If there is one area of business I see butchered the most, and one area of business people seek help in the least, it's self-introduction.

I'd estimate that in my 45-plus years of business, I've heard over 100,000 self-introductions (you might have heard them called elevator pitches). In 2008, I heard over 10,000 (yes, I tracked them). You might say I've heard it all.

Imagine you're going to invest in a commercial you'll

run on television, radio, or even on social media platforms like Facebook. Would you fire up the camera and microphone and say whatever fell out of your mouth? I would hope not.

You'd probably think long and hard about who you want to talk to, what you want them to hear from you, what you hope to accomplish, and how you'll say it to make that happen. And while that's better, it's still not best. While this book won't cover this topic in detail, the following will provide an excellent foundation.

Earlier, we discussed your Statement of Value, Ideal Customer Identity, and Ideal Customer Association List. To recap, these are the "what I do," "who I do it for," and "who knows who I do it for" statements. These will be essential in creating the various ways you'll introduce yourself.

Here's what I learned: When promoting yourself either through self-introduction or advertising, it's essential to think about what the person hearing you wants. Even the needs of the prospective target of your message are secondary to wants. You must determine what your prospect feels and how you hope to make her feel. You must take her from feeling she has a deficiency in some way to feeling you and your product can make her feel fulfilled.

What's more, I learned that I need to have several versions of my self-introduction to deliver in different settings. What I say in front of a large crowd is different from what I say one-on-one. And I also learned that, while I may be talking about myself, my company, and what we can do to help a target client, it needs to be memorable in a way that the people I meet can pass on to the people they meet.

POWER TIP: You have to talk about the product of the product. Too many people talk about their product or service and fail to talk about what happens to the customer when they use it. No one cares about you or your product until they know it can do something for them they cannot do for themselves.

Here's what I did: I experimented quite a bit on what worked and what didn't. I created and rehearsed in front of a mirror my 60-second, 30-second, and 7-second self-introduction. I identified my target prospect, thought about her wants and needs, thought about how she feels, and then developed a message that said to her how I could make her feel better.

Once I had the words I wanted to say, I concentrated on how I would say them. There is a certain level of theatrics necessary to stand out from the crowd. And how you say what you say may communicate more than the message you've crafted.

One of the biggest problems I see with self-introductions is lack of confidence. Because people don't know what to say or how to say it, they stammer and twitch and just look like an amateur.

Having an actual script and rehearsing in front of a mirror until you have it down cold ensures you'll appear confident. This is your profession. Treat it as a professional would. Rehearse until you know the words intuitively, and then rehearse in front of a mirror until you know the exact gestures you'll use with each word.

Actually, if you think about television commercials, you can find examples of them where no words are used and the message is communicated.

There's a Michelob Ultra commercial from some years ago that shows a young man and woman who apparently do not know each other. They're working out in a health club, then running past each other in a park, and then meeting in a bar and both having a Michelob Ultra. The message? Drink our beer, get the girl or guy.

Here's what to do: You'll need to do this with all versions of your self-introduction. Write out the script. Practice it in front of a mirror. Record yourself with video and watch not only what you say but how you say it. Gestures need to be congruent. Watch for action words in the script and put gestures with them that match. If you say "You," put your hands out faceup toward the crowd.

Here's what not to do: Avoid "I," "we," and other personal references and rewrite to say "you" and other references to the listener.

One of the best examples I can give is of my friend Arthur Fessenden (ArtofCruising.com). Arthur taught me that you just have to do you the way you feel naturally, or it just won't work. He always ends his self-introduction by saying his "services are free." I begged him to drop that part of his introduction and promotion, but it just is so much a part of him, he seems less genuine without it. He's traveled to more than 125 countries, and since he's so genuine and so interested in other people, he has friends in ports of call all over the world that he can rely on to help his clients have a magnificent time when they travel.

Arthur Fessenden, owner, ArtofCruising.com

But one thing we were able to change about Arthur's self-introduction was the way he built credibility. He used to say, "I'm affiliated with the largest travel agency in the world." While this does lend credibility, it does nothing to say why that matters to the listener. We changed it to, "My affiliation with the largest travel agency in the world gives you access to benefits and amenities you just can't find anywhere else." Now, the credibility is communicated in a way that matters to the listener.

POWER TIP: You have only 3 seconds. When I first started studying and developing my self-introduction, people said you have about 7 seconds to get someone's attention before he or she moves on mentally. But new studies have shown the attention you get is limited to 3 seconds now. Make the beginning count! To learn more about what to say and how to say it, visit MillionDollarMeetings.com.

CHAPTER 21:

What to say and when to say it

In chamber meetings as in everyday life, what you say and how you say it matters. I believe that you are responsible for what the other person hears, not just what you say. That's important to understand.

What you say is what you believe people hear. But what people hear can be far different from what you have said. How you say it, what they expect to hear, your gestures, facial expressions, and even the environment around you all play a part in what people will hear when you speak to them.

So, it is best that you focus on what you want the other person to hear, not just what you will say.

We've discussed a lot about what you will say. Your Statement of Value, Your Ideal Customer Identity, and your Ideal Customer Association List will form much of that. Now let's discuss what you'll say in different situations and how you will say it.

Essentially there are three different scenarios where you'll need to answer the question, "What do you do?"

1. In a sit-down meeting or meal one-on-one (with an individual)
2. In a presentation-style meeting with a structured self-introduction component
3. In a casual meeting, cocktail or after-hours, or other less-structured meet and greet

Of course there will be variations of each, but the essential elements are usually the same. Let's break down each.

One-on-one or other sit-down
meeting with an individual

This meeting is more interview than introduction. It is usually informal and open to flow as your styles permit. If you deliver a canned, prepared, and rehearsed self-introduction in this environment, you'll be quickly dismissed as salesy, self-absorbed, and insincere. It's essential you don't let this happen, even if you determine you don't have a connection with this person, because you never know who they may know that you need to know.

The best way to ensure you'll be sincere and genuine is to ask a lot of questions. Usually, the questions you ask will be asked back of you, so be prepared to answer them. Usually, you'll have some frame knowledge of the person you are meeting with since this is a one-on-one, but sometimes at chamber events, they'll structure impromptu one-on-one meetings. The best advice is, just be you. Eventually, if you are to do business with or become referral partners with the person you are meeting, you'll have to like each other. If you've been someone you aren't, once they get to know you, they'll really feel betrayed. Just be you.

Presentation Style Meeting
with a Self-Introduction Component

If there is ever a time to be someone you are not, this is it. Not to say you should be fake, but you should be larger than life to some degree. This is the time when you are on stage, so remember, "It's showtime!"

This is the type of self-introduction where you (and everyone else in the room) has between fifteen seconds and one minute to stand and introduce yourself and your company. Full detail of these kinds of mini-presentations is beyond the scope of this book, but here is a six-step guide to better self-introductions of this type.

1. As the introductions go around the room and get to the person next to you, push your chair back from the table when the person next to you pushes their chair back.

This eliminates awkward noises, delays, and the possibility of your not being ready when it is your turn. If you are seated at the end of a table, be sure to push your chair back from the table immediately when the meeting starts. You might be called on first!

2. Stand up. Even if every person in the room hasn't done so, you should stand. Standing gives you the authority position in the room. It also gives you proper posture for presenting.

3. Pause. Don't speak right away. There are two reasons for this. First, many in the audience will still be thinking about what the prior person said. You need to give them a moment to focus on you. Second, we are uncomfortable with silence. People expect you to begin immediately. If you don't, they'll look up to see what's going on, and you've got their attention.

4. Take a deep breath. This is essential because you'll need that air to deliver your message. But taking a deep breath also provides a calming effect.

5. Lean slightly forward. When we tell a secret, we lean in. Leaning in closes the gap between you and your audience. I suggest you just put your weight on the front part of your feet, as if you were anticipating a serve in tennis. This way you're more balanced and prepared for movement. Try it. It works.

6. Speak louder than you think you have to. I'm not suggesting you scream, but remember there are people in the back of the room who may not be able to hear you at your normal tone. Slightly louder than you think you have to speak will do the trick. It will also ensure you don't sound timid. Timid people aren't often believable.

For more ideas and techniques on presentation-style self-introductions, visit MillionDollarMeetings.com.

A casual or cocktail meeting self-introduction

You've probably been there before. You're at an after-hours, cocktail party, backyard barbecue, or even in the checkout line at the grocery store. A conversation starts, and before long you're asked, "So, what do you do for a living?"

This is not the time to trot out your prepared self-introduction or your Statement of Value. That will seem way too structured and will sound like a commercial. You don't want to do that. Not cool.

Instead, let it flow like a real conversation. After all, that's what you're having, isn't it?

But sometimes you need a crutch. Something to fall back on when the words aren't coming and the conversation isn't flowing. Here's your crutch. It's what I call the

"Have you ever" technique.

Someone asks you, "So Mary, what do you do?" You reply, "Have you ever come home to a hot house in the summer because the A/C went out?" (Wait for the nod or reply yes.) "I help make sure that doesn't happen again." Obviously, Mary is in the heating and air conditioning business.

When I attend events for our dry cleaning delivery service and I'm asked what I do, I say, "Have you ever put your clothes in the car to take them to the cleaners and then driven around with them in the car for a couple of days or weeks? I make sure that doesn't happen to you."

Think about what you do and how it eliminates a key problem for your target customer. Then just make it into a "Have you ever" statement.

CHAPTER 22

Beyond the words you use

I've heard that more than 60 percent of statistics are made up on the spot. This one is not. Depending on what you read and where you read it, anywhere from 70 percent to 93 percent of all communication is nonverbal.

Most people are aware that nonverbal means body language, eye contact, gestures, and posture. But it can mean a lot more than that. It also means how and when you enter or leave a room, how you approach people, and how you disengage.

So, it stands to reason you'll need some pointers on the nonverbal skills necessary to succeed in getting your message out and being known as someone who others want to meet, talk with, and ultimately build a relationship with. Here are just a few, and more can be found at MillionDolllarMeetings.com.

1. Look into my eyes. Everyone knows eye contact is important. But you may not know that men and women are different in their need for it. Men need only about 3 seconds of eye-to-eye contact to feel they are being heard and appreciated. Women need a lot more, and some studies say it is as much as 17 seconds of dedicated eye contact. So look more directly, especially with women.

   As for where to look, depending on how close you are, it's easiest and best to look at the bridge of the nose. Not the nose, because people are sensitive about their noses, but at the bridge. Most people won't be able to tell you aren't looking at their eyes unless you're really close. Then, choose one eye and focus on it. Try not to go back and forth between eyes because that can be misinterpreted as shifty.

2. Stand up straight, shoulders back now. Whether you're seated or standing, your torso should be erect. It's easy to find yourself slouching, and when you do, remind yourself to stand or sit up. This isn't just for the others in the room, it's for you as well. When you use proper posture, you feel better, more confident, and more in control. And as an added benefit, your diaphragm won't be compressed, making it harder to breathe and speak effectively.

3. Here's what to do with your arms and hands. Of course,

it's best if you don't cross your arms (or your legs for that matter), but also be aware and resist the temptation to "talk with your hands" too much. Relaxed and at your side is best when it comes to control of your arms. If you do feel the need to move your hands, be certain to make motions that complement what you are saying. Don't say, "Go over there" and motion toward a different direction.

4. Know how to shake hands. A firm, web-to-web handshake is perfect. We've all been victim of the over-the-top, excessively firm handshake that leaves us in pain, and we've all suffered the awkwardness of a handshake that didn't make it all the way into the hand. Do your best to get the base of your thumb and forefinger to meet up with the other person's. Then, a firm-but-not-too-firm squeeze, and not for too long either. You'll know if you held on too long if the other person disengages first. Remember that next time.

5. Smile! I cannot emphasize this enough. We all tend to spend most of our days thinking. A thinking face is not a smiling face. But people are attracted to a smile. When you're smiling, it says you're friendly and open to conversation. You'll do more business, meet more interesting people, make more money, and ultimately have a better life if you just focus on smiling more often. Try it.

6. Dress the part. A number of years ago, I was hosting the member orientation at the Metro Atlanta Chamber. A little over 100 people were in the room, and as you might expect at a major city chamber orientation, most of them were wearing business attire. Men in suits, women in suits or dresses, all mostly black, navy, or other dark colors that say, "Take me seriously. I sure do."

I strongly urge you to dress one level better than you think you have to at most meetings and you'll never be uncomfortable. But there is an exception. If you are in a trade or job that people associate with a particular uniform, always wear your uniform. As an example, at this meeting there was a painter who came dressed in his painting clothes. White shirt, white pants, tennis shoes, all covered in paint splatter. You knew exactly what he did. And he received more leads and referrals that day than anyone else. Dress the part and you'll always win.

7. More than a business card: Do I have to remind you to bring your business cards? Probably not at this point, but you might be tempted to bring and hand out promotional materials at events. Just remember two things. First, most people won't be in the market for your services right now, and second, most people won't want your promotional material right now. That doesn't mean there isn't a place for it, just keep it in the car or

at your desk and give it out only when asked to or when you have a conversation that will be enhanced by the item. Never distribute without permission. And always pick up any pieces that are left behind. If you don't, they'll just be thrown away.

8. Be on time. Yes, there will be times when something unavoidable will come up and you'll still want to go the meeting, but you should always endeavor to be on time. If it happens that you're late, by all means, enter without fanfare or making an issue of it. Everyone knows you're late, so don't bring attention to it. Enter quietly.

   Being on time means arriving at least fifteen minutes before the function starts. That's because some of the best connections you can make will happen before the meeting even starts (remember my Steve Forbes story from page 77.)

   Everyone who arrives early is looking for someone to talk to and who is like they are—uncomfortable. When you walk up and say "Hi" with a smile, the nervousness leaves and you've made a friend. Remember, friends do business with friends.

9. Do what you say you'll do. Remember when I mentioned that you are responsible for what people hear? Here's a big tip: Never say "Maybe" or "I'll try." Never say, "I hope to see you again" or "Maybe we'll see each other

again" when you don't really plan to. "Maybe" and "I'll try" sound like you will to the listener. If you make a promise, even unintentionally, follow up and follow through.

10. Invite a guest. You'll find people will be more interested in you when you invite someone to attend a meeting. It shows you're interested in promoting others, not just you. When you do, make sure to introduce them to someone who needs to meet them too.

11. Attend regularly. Determine the type of event and time of day that works for you and attend regularly. People get familiar with people they see often, and hearing what you do and how you do it over and over will build familiarity. Being there all the time keeps you top of mind.

12. Stay late. Don't leave early. Just like getting there early gives you access to people, so does staying late. As the meeting winds down or ends, people will naturally want to converse about what's been said and what they heard. It's a great time for you to be asked about what you do or to ask others and get more detail.

Finally, while it's been said before, be yourself. There's no reason to try to be someone you aren't, because eventually, you'll have a relationship with the people you meet, and when you do, you'll have to remember who they think you are that they like. It's impossible.

Get people to like you as you are. There are plenty of people in the world who will like you for who you are, so don't sweat it.

CHAPTER 23

Nothing Kills Success Like A Little Success

The nature of chamber membership is cyclical. Here's what I mean.

Most people join a chamber because they're looking for more business or personal fulfillment. When they achieve it, they become too busy to go to the chamber and get more out of it. So, since they aren't constantly filling their pipeline with new business or with new experiences that are fulfilling, success begins to dwindle.

When it does, they go back to the chamber, and the cycle happens again. Unfortunately, after a few times, most people begin to believe the chamber isn't working for them. Actually, the chamber worked too well for them, and they weren't ready for success.

You have to have a plan in place to support the business you are going to be bringing in. If you aren't ready for growth, you won't continue to grow.

As your business grows by the nature of your chamber involvement, so too will the number of people who expect to do business directly with you. You must plan for this now. How will you move people from meeting you to working with someone on your team?

Here's what I learned: People expect that they'll work with the people they meet at events and build relationships with. If you don't have a plan for this, it will stifle growth and prevent further success.

Here's what I did: In the beginning, I learned this lesson the hard way, and it almost killed our business. When you are the marketing, sales, service, management, accounting, and customer service department in your firm, it can be overwhelming. Later I learned to outsource the tasks I wasn't particularly skilled in and to focus on the ones I was.

In our business, that started with my wife and sons doing the pickup and delivery of dry cleaning while I was out marketing and selling. Then, I was pulled back into the service end because we grew so fast. That stopped growth. Today, we are always looking for a new hire because we're aware that we're growing and will need someone soon. Looking before we need someone eliminates what we've done way too many times, hire the first person who seemed like a winner instead of waiting to find the right person who is a winner.

Here's what to do: Even if you are a solopreneur, be on the watch for people you can employ as your business grows. In the beginning, this will mean finding people who can do tasks better than you can do them yourself. If you fall behind in bookkeeping, contract with a bookkeeper rather than hire someone as an employee. Your costs will be kept down, and you'll always have expert help.

And right now, begin documenting every process in your business. This way you can easily integrate a new hire or a contractor into your business. Instead of having to explain everything over and over, you'll be able to explain it once and then have them refer to the process sheet or manual for that part of your business.

CHAPTER 24

Understanding the Real Value

You likely already know about lifetime value in business. You probably even know the lifetime value of a customer or client in your business.

There's also a lifetime value in knowledge. Something you learn today and use over and over later in life may make or save you millions. I hope this book will too.

Here are a few examples of things I learned along the way that made a tremendous difference in my life.

During my work with chambers, I got the opportunity to attend the Georgia Academy of Economic Development. What I learned there has been incredibly valuable to my business.

Not only did I learn about how communities can attract

or repel potential investment, but I also learned how site selectors choose one community over another.

But here's the real deal. It's not how they choose, it's how they exclude that matters. Site selectors will visit communities unannounced. They'll shop in shops, eat at restaurants, drive the roads at rush hour, and drive around neighborhoods and schools. They'll check out a community thoroughly before they even consider it.

And what they do is astounding. They're looking for any reason to exclude a community from consideration. That's right, they don't look for what they like. They look for what they don't like.

POWER TIP: Remember, people have thousands of decisions to make every day. They are more likely to eliminate your business from consideration than to include it for consideration. Be aware of the things your company does and says that might set it up for exclusion—and eliminate all you can.

I worked on a community branding campaign with Linda Mosely at 365 Degree Total Marketing. She and her team showed me how colors and shapes can impact the way people see your brand, company, or community. They also showed me the power of listening to what people say they want, guiding them to what they need, and finding the middle ground.

POWER TIP: The client isn't always right. There are things the client doesn't know and can't possibly know that will hurt them, and it's your job, the expert's job, to make sure the client gets what she needs while considering what she wants. If she can't be swayed, she can't be helped.

I also learned from many, many experiences that people really do want the best. While people say they want the cheapest, or the quickest, or the smallest, they really want what's best. Most of the time people will settle for less only because they don't know they can have something better.

POWER TIP: People will resist saying what they want because they don't believe they can have it. It's your job to get out of them what they really want and then to show them how they can have it.

People just have to believe and they'll be able to do most anything.

One day I was doing an orientation at the Metro Atlanta Chamber. Let me set the scene.

The room was on the second floor of the chamber. The chamber building was downtown and overlooked Centennial Olympic Park, site of the 1996 Centennial Olympic Games. When I say "overlooked," I mean the entire length of the room was one big glass window overlooking the park and much of downtown Atlanta. It was a wonderful venue.

Metro Atlanta Chamber building 2006

The room was packed with business leaders and wannabes. All were there to make their mark, meet the right person, or somehow improve their business lives. But from my experience doing this program, I knew they could improve not only their business lives but also their personal lives as well.

> **POWER TIP:** People don't really want success or money, they want what they think success or money will do for them. They want the product of the product.

I had done two orientations at the MAC prior. Both were as they had been done before I got there. I followed the script. But this time, I tried something different.

I kept the curtains closed until the very end. Then, just before I wrapped up, I had the curtains open to reveal that beautiful park and skyline. Next, I asked everyone to get up and walk to the window (very much like Robin Williams' character did with the trophy case in Dead Poets Society).

"Please, come closer. Get right up to the glass or as close as you can. Look out there. What do you see?" (Silence). "That, ladies and gentlemen, is your dream. It's right out there, waiting for you to admit you have it, admit you want it, and admit you deserve it. When you're ready to live your dream, the Metro Atlanta Chamber and I are ready to help you. And we can. Thanks for being here today. My name is Glen Gould, and I hope you'll admit your dream and act on it today."

At first, dead silence. No applause like normal. I thought I had blown it. Then, they just started talking with each other. I heard one say, "Yeah. Why not?" And then I heard someone looking out at the skyline say, "I'm gonna make you my bitch." Everyone laughed, they clapped, and they had a great time.

POWER TIP: Try something so unexpected that you just might fail. You might be surprised how successful you'll be.

CHAPTER 25

It's About People: How One Introduction Changes Lives

While it may be hard to put a dollar figure or lifetime estimate on the value of experiences, it is impossible to put a dollar figure or lifetime value on relationships. And while I'm not advocating you do, you need to understand that the real value of chamber membership is in the people you meet and the relationships you create. It's been said, "If you don't like people, you've got a real problem because that's all we have around here."

In this section, I'll tell a few stories of some of the people I've met along the way and what they've meant to me. In doing so, I hope you'll find that what you're looking for might be closer than you think. It just might be one person away.

Tim Gargis is my friend. One of my closest friends,

even though we don't see each other very often. We have a bond. Tim is a sales manager at the Georgia Tech Global Learning Center. We met at the Metro Atlanta Chamber of Commerce.

One day, Tim introduced me to Buddy Estes. Buddy was an Allstate Insurance agency owner. Buddy and I became friends, and the three of would get together from time to time.

Buddy introduced me to Mark Spackman, who introduced me to Carlyle Kaufmann, who ultimately introduced me to the Atlanta Regional office of Subway. I've spoken to this group four times with over 100 people in the audience at Coca-Cola Headquarters. A really cool gig. You can see a video of one of the meetings at https://goo.gl/ukcZKk.

Me preparing to present at Coca-Cola Headquarters

When I lost my job at the MAC, Buddy, Tim, and I would get together less often, but each year around Christmas, we'd meet for lunch. Buddy and Tim always brought a small present, and I always felt like a heel because I didn't. Then I moved away, and the connection became more on-line than in person.

One year we weren't able to meet for Christmastime lunch. Buddy's dad had been in and out of the hospital for the better part of a year with cancer, and Buddy just couldn't break away. I suggested we get together and play golf sometime in the spring. It was late summer before we did. Buddy's dad was in really bad shape, and they were going to consider taking him off life support soon.

That day was amazing. Buddy played better than he ever had. We laughed, we cried, we bonded again. And for the first time in a long time, Buddy had a day where he wasn't overwhelmed by the thought of his dad dying.

We hugged in the parking lot and committed to not let so much time go by without getting together again.

The following week, I called Buddy to check in with him and see how his dad was. His wife answered the phone and said, "Hi, Glen, this is Tamara. Buddy passed away this morning." Confused by what I'd just heard, I assumed Buddy's dad had died. I said, "Oh, please tell Buddy I'm sorry and to call me when he can."

How Tamara did it, I'll never know, but she restated, "No, Glen, Buddy died this morning."

"What? How? That's not possible. Buddy isn't supposed to die, James is!"

There's more to the story, but to sum it up, I'll simply say this. Tim and I are friends forever. We both loved Buddy. My son played golf with us that day, and he now knows firsthand how fragile life is too.

It's changed us. We miss him. When we drive by his gravesite, we're reminded that life is short, life is precious. Don't let life go by without doing what you want to because one day you might not get to. What would have happened if we hadn't played golf that day? I can't imagine. That's a lesson you just can't unlearn. And I learned it because I met Tim, and he introduced me to Buddy.

CHAPTER 26

The Atlanta Community Breakfast: Access and Lessons Learned

Phil Kratovil was on a mission (and he still is). He wants to spread the good news of Jesus. He attended every chamber event he could, promoting the Atlanta Community Breakfast as a place where "we discuss faith and values in the workplace."

Phil Kratovil, Atlanta Community Breakfast

I attended a few of the breakfasts and always had ideas for Phil about how he could make it better. Phil had been running it for years, and it was an integral part of his job working for Carver College. It was an outreach ministry to attract donors, mentors, and students to the college.

About a year later, Phil took a new position in Washington and left the ACB in my hands. And from this one connection through the chamber, I met some amazing people and learned a lot.

First, I was immediately in contact with Dan Cathy of Chick-fil-A. Dan spoke at one of the breakfasts, and when I asked him how I should introduce him, he simply said, "Tell them my name is Dan and I'm in customer service." You might think that was just being clever or humble, but actually it was both and neither. You see, Dan Cathy really is just "Dan in customer service." That's how he sees his role. That's how everyone sees their role at Chick-fil-A. It's all about serving the customer.

Dan Cathy, CEO of Chick-fil-A

Power Tip: Everyone is in customer service. We exist to serve others and in doing so we serve ourselves.

I also met and spent time with former Atlanta Falcons and Denver Broncos Head Coach Dan Reeves. I learned how to deal with people who have tremendous egos and salaries far greater than my own.

Coach Reeves told stories about working with young men who, months earlier, had little to no income and suddenly had found wealth. A professional football player might make ten times the amount his coach does, and this can cause the ego to be inflated. Not only that, he also has physical strength and stamina in abundance.

He said you have to have empathy for them. You have to really care. Not just for what they do on the field, or off the field as it relates to their performance, but what happens in their everyday lives. What happens to them when they are on top and what will happen to them when they aren't. Because everyone eventually isn't on top any longer, especially in professional football.

Coach Reeves really cared about his men. He cared about their lives, personally, professionally, and spiritually. I presume he still does.

POWER TIP: Remember that no one is on top

forever. Remember that everyone essentially wants the same thing you do—a good life, caring friends and family, and significance to those who matter most to them.

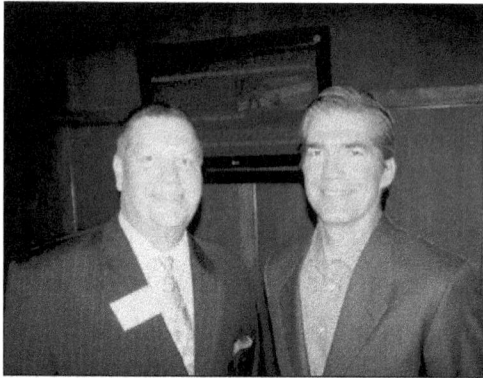

Me and Joel Manby, former CEO of
Herschend Family Entertainment

Joel Manby spoke at the Atlanta Community Breakfast. He was the CEO of Herschend Family Entertainment when I met him. Dollywood and Stone Mountain Park are a couple of properties they manage. He was featured on the television show *Undercover Boss*. Joel taught me about the value of values in corporate America and the power of forgiveness.

He was late to his interview with Jack Herschend, a man who is extremely punctual. Joel said, "He saw being late as a form of disrespect. But he forgave me and gave me another chance."

That forgiveness is a principle in the way Joel Manby

leads people.

> **POWER TIP:** Have standards but don't be inflexible. You just might find your best asset is to forgive people who don't know what is important to you until you tell them it is.

I met Shane Thompson, founder of Shane's Rib Shack, by contacting the corporate office and asking him to speak at the Atlanta Community Breakfast. Shane is a down-to-earth person who hasn't forgotten his roots. He taught me about following your dream and using what you have to the fullest.

Shane's first Rib Shack was just that, a shack. Hence the name. But he had many things going for him including a good work ethic, family support, and a clear focus on his dream.

It didn't hurt that his grandfather, "Big Dad," had a killer BBQ recipe either.

> **POWER TIP:** You have your own secret recipe. Don't hide it. Put it front and center and believe in your dream.

I met so many wonderful people and influential leaders through the ACB, it is a shame I can't mention them all. They all added to my success.

But perhaps the biggest lesson I learned through the Atlanta Community Breakfast was that if you don't give it your all, if you aren't all in, no matter how good the product or the cause, it will fail.

Sadly, I wasn't prepared to give the ACB my all. It wasn't my full-time focus, and because it wasn't, I tried to make it good enough. Good enough never is.

At first it was the quality of the meetings that started to suffer. I couldn't plan well enough to make them dynamic, and they became ordinary. In an effort to make them better, I moved from once a week to once a month. That eliminated the predictability of the event, and people became involved in other things.

As a last effort, I changed the venue. But that meant that people who were used to going one place that was convenient for them found it difficult to get to the new place. I had essentially killed it.

POWER TIP: If you aren't all in, you better be ready to find something else to do, because when you aren't giving it your all, it can't give you all you want in return.

CHAPTER 27:

Other Influencers I Met Along The Way

Al Lautenslager is a professional speaker, consultant, and best-selling author of many books, including *Guerrilla Marketing in 30 Days*. Al taught me to be a self-promoter. I invited him to speak at the Metro Atlanta Chamber, and his presentation was great.

One of the tips he shared that day that I still use to this day is to be a self-promoter. For example, he was speaking at the time we were promoting our Small Business Person of the Year program and urging people to nominate themselves and others. Al suggested that you nominate yourself for businessperson of the year.

POWER TIP: I'll paraphrase his suggestion.

Here's what you should do. Nominate yourself for Small Business Person of the Year. Take a picture of yourself outside the chamber building. Make sure the logo is in the picture. Then, get the image and the "Nominated for Small Business Person of the Year" artwork from the chamber (we would give that to anyone who was nominated). Take the picture, the "nominated" graphic, and create a press release saying that you've been nominated. Send it out to PRWeb and the local media. Then send it to anyone and everyone you know. Your friends, colleagues, employees, business associates, vendors, and yes, most importantly, your clients and customers. Who knows, you just might win. And don't forget to put it on your website and marketing materials. Brilliant, just brilliant.

Tana Goertz is a former contestant on *The Apprentice* and a professional speaker. She also worked on Donald Trump's successful bid for the presidency. Tana taught me to be memorable and to do things no one else is willing to do. I met Tana through a mutual acquaintance, Danita Harn of Harn and Associates Back Office Solutions.

Tana sent me an introduction packet unlike any I had ever seen. It was a small, personalized metal tin, and inside were promotional photos, a biography, and among other things, a disc with her "sizzle reel." At a time when most speakers were sending an email asking to speak, Tana sent something tangible that I couldn't ignore.

So, of course, I had her speak at the Metro Atlanta Chamber. Even though I had seen her on *The Apprentice*, to hear her tell the story of bedazzling garments to sell them was a real eye-opener.

She also taught me that experience in a previous life might just be super-valuable in a new life. The Bedazzler was something she had used years before she came up with the idea to use it on *The Apprentice*.

POWER TIP: Do a little more than is expected and you can expect bigger and better results. In a world where everyone is the same, be different. What works in one field may not be familiar in another, so bring your past experiences and use them.

Lori Ruff is the LinkedIn Diva. She is a Forbes Top 10 Social Media Power Influencer. She taught me about the power of LinkedIn.com and how to create credibility through your LinkedIn profile. She showed me that using your LinkedIn profile, you can compete with a company of any size and win.

Lori Ruff, The LinkedIn Diva presenting at the Newnan-Coweta Chamber

She explained that LinkedIn was the place where people vetted you without you knowing it. This was in 2009, and it's still true today. If you didn't have a LinkedIn profile, you would automatically be discounted. It's a prerequisite for business.

She also taught me to #keepitreal. She didn't make a big deal about it back then, she just was so genuine you couldn't help but be compelled to realize that being you is about the best you'll ever do. So be you.

POWER TIP: Don't ignore LinkedIn and other social media. They aren't going away. If you can't keep up with it, hire someone who will. But don't delegate and walk away. Social media is social, so as Lori would say, "Keep It Real."

Mike O'Neil is the founder of Integrated Alliances (IntegratedAlliances.com) and the LinkedIn Rock Star. Mike taught me about big data before big data was even a big term. His understanding of what was and is happening in the world of big data and social media is unmatched.

Mike O'Neil, The LinkedIn Rock Star presenting at the Newnan-Coweta Chamber

He talked about how knowing more about your target audience than anyone else will pay big and that one sure-fire way to know your audience is to attract them with something you have in common. In his case, he used his love—and that of many of his clients and prospects—for rock-and-roll music. Together with Lori Ruff, he wrote *Rock The World with Social Media*.

POWER TIP: Build in ways to learn about your clients as you attract them. Have a new client questionnaire and ask for things like birthdays, spouse names, and hobbies. The more you know about your client, the more they'll like you.

Their book explained how to super-charge your LinkedIn profile and social media presence while tying the lessons to stories of rock legends and concerts. You might like to check it out. https://goo.gl/E14kii

Lori Ruff, me, and Mike O'Neil at the Metro Atlanta Chamber

Steve Kaplan is an entrepreneur, business development guru, best-selling author of three books including *Bag the Elephant!* and a Tony Award nominee for Best Musical. You could say Steve's a master of many trades.

I had Steve speak shortly after his book *Bag the Elephant!* was released. He's a great speaker, and the audience loved him, especially since he had firsthand experience of going after big business and becoming one too. He taught me that you have to identify who the target is and learn everything you can about their needs so you can become the perfect solution to their problems.

Steve Kaplan, author of *Bag The Elephant!* at the Metro Atlanta Chamber

He also taught me about persistence. Early in his career, he realized Procter & Gamble was the ideal client for him, so he persisted until he got his first opportunity there. Five years later, he was working with over 50 of the P&G brands.

POWER TIP: Big companies can lead to big opportunities. When I was in the retail store maintenance business, I would piggyback on one store to get to another, then from district and region to district and region while using my references from within the company in order to grow. Big companies are worth the effort.

Jim Dawson is a professional speaker, author of *101 Prospecting Nuggets* and *101 Speaking Nuggets*, and the founder of ADI Marketing.

Jim taught me, really taught me, about communicating effectively. It's not just what you say, it's how you say it. I'll never forget his pointing out to me that I put my hands out when I was saying "Come here." It's a total disconnect and showed that I had written the words and rehearsed them, but I hadn't really become them.

Jim Dawson, ADI Performance

If you want people to come to you, you motion toward you, not away. He also taught me how to introduce a speaker to an audience. If you're going to introduce someone, you have to set the tone. Even if you're reading a bio, you have to give it energy. And at the end, slightly raising your voice and prompting the crowd to clap by clapping gives the speaker a good start. Everyone needs a good start.

And Jim also taught me the power of storytelling. You need to tell a story in order to get people to listen to you.

POWER TIP: Tell a story about how you helped someone with your service or product. That's always better than telling someone what your product does.

James Roland is the owner of The Perfect Caper, a gourmet restaurant in Punta Gorda, Florida (thePerfectCaper. com). James was the chair of the Punta Gorda Chamber when I was president, and he taught me to think really big.

He had the original idea for a wine festival in Punta Gorda. After Hurricane Charley, I championed the idea because we needed a way to bring people to the city, have them spend their money, but then leave since we had almost no hotel rooms left.

When James and I first started talking about his wine festival, I jokingly said we should have a big national act come. One of us suggested Spyro Gyra, one of the biggest jazz bands of all time. We had no money, no draw, and no hope, but James said, "Why not?" Why not indeed.

It wasn't that hard to find their agent. It was even easier to book them. Once we had Spyro Gyra booked, it was amazingly easy to get people on board and to sponsor and promote the festival.

POWER TIP: Find something that people can't do on their own, show them how you can help them do it, and you'll get all the help you need to pull it off.

My family with Spyro Gyra after the
Inaugural Punta Gorda Wine Festival

It's been over 13 years since the first Punta Gorda Wine Festival, and now, the Punta Gorda Wine and Jazz Festival is a can't-miss event each February. Check it out: https://puntagordachamber.com/product/14th-annu-al-wine-jazz-festival-2019/

Patrick McGaughey is a speaker and trainer and former chamber executive. He taught me to be bold.

Shortly after I started as president of the Punta Gorda Chamber, I attended my first Florida Association of Chamber Professionals meeting. Pat was a presenter. He did a lot to be memorable, but I was more impressed by his boldness.

Power Tip: Just because you don't use an idea the way it was intended doesn't mean it doesn't have value. Be bold!

Here's an example. Many chambers give new members a plaque to hang on their wall or a sticker to put on the front door. This shows the public they are a member, and according to surveys, people are 68 percent more likely to do business with a chamber member than with a non-chamber member.

Patrick McGaughey presenting at the NuLink Early Bird Forum

You've probably seen it. A peeling sticker or a tired, dusty plaque dated ten years ago at an establishment you frequent that hasn't renewed their membership. Pat suggested that, if a member didn't renew, we should go in and demand our plaque back or to even carry a window scraper and scrape the decal off the door. He felt it made both the former member and the chamber look bad.

Hey, when your customer quits being your customer, what right do they have to claim they still are? In full disclosure, while I loved the idea, I never followed through on it. But it did serve as a constant reminder to always be bold.

Jim Kill is a professional sales trainer and teacher. Jim taught me what a professional sales person does and looks like.

When we first met, he pulled out a form and said that we would "learn a little about you, learn a little about me, and see if we have a fit." Everything he did was professional. If he said he'd call me at 11 a.m. on Thursday, my phone rang at 11 a.m. His dress, demeanor, and approach were confidently friendly.

POWER TIP: Everyone is in sales. Even if you aren't selling a product or service for profit, you're selling yourself every day. You're even selling yourself on yourself.

Jim's Natural Selling Concepts program is aptly named because everything he did and everything he teaches focuses on being who and what you are naturally. If you work for a sales organization or if you are in selling, I highly recommend you take his course. https://www.stellarsales.com/contact.php

Helene Lollis taught me that successful people and leaders read.

POWER TIP: I hate to read, so while Helene reads a lot and she shared many titles with me, I never really read them. I chose to listen on audiobook. If you don't like to read but need to keep informed, I recommend using Audible.com.

Helene also showed me how to effectively lead a group of volunteers. Her company, Pathbuilders, uses corporate women who are leaders in their fields as mentors to up-and-coming women. It's a brilliant business model, and it helps so many become more successful.

She also taught me about marketing, while not directly. She suggested I read Made to Stick by Chip Heath and Dan Heath. It is perfectly named because it teaches you why and how messages "stick" and spread. Again, I listened to the audiobook, but either way, it is fantastic. You should check it out.

Jay Ordan is a serial entrepreneur who taught me the importance of a consistent brand, regardless of the size of your company. Not only does it communicate professionalism, but it also shows that you have given thought to who you are and what you do. And in doing so, you've learned more about your company and your target client. The fact that you look like one of the "big boys" doesn't hurt either.

> **Power Tip:** What you say about your brand needs to be consistent. Everything is marketing and marketing is everything.

These and many other people I've met along the way remain very dear friends. My life is richer because of our relationship.

CHAPTER 28:

Be Prepared For What Most People Do

There are so many people who have shared with me wisdom and experience, it saddens me I cannot recall them all by name. But those above are just some examples of what you can learn at a chamber.

But the overall theme I learned from every interaction with every person at a chamber was the idea that I could be more, do more, have more, give more, and ultimately live more.

And so I hope that we are now more than acquaintances. I hope we are friends. And since we've met through the chamber, so to speak, I'd like to share a story with you of one more of my experiences that will help you.

In 2007, Ben Turpin and I wrote *Meet Me At Starbucks*. Unlike other books we had written, this book was written with a specific purpose.

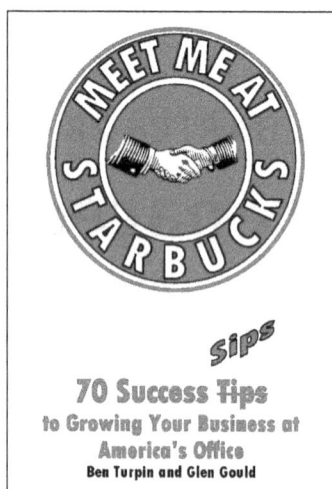

Meet Me At Starbucks book cover.

Earlier in our work together, Ben would come to the point in the program where he'd say, "So, you call up the person you met last night and ask him or her to meet you at Starbucks for a cup of coffee." Ben loves Starbucks. No, really, he loves it.

One day someone came to the stage after the event and asked if we were sponsored by Starbucks. Surprisingly, it hadn't entered either one of our minds that we might be able to get a sponsorship from them. And that started the idea train.

What if we wrote a book about meeting someone at Starbucks? Yeah, that would work, right? Then we really turned it up a notch.

Ben knew hundreds of people who worked at Starbucks in Florida. He knew or had a connection to several area managers and district managers. And of course, we knew that Howard Schultz was the founder. It didn't take much work to get names, addresses, and even the birthday of Howard Schultz. Then, we created our plan. Let's see if you can find the flaw in it.

We'd write a book titled *Meet Me At Starbucks*. We'd rip off their logo, change it a bit to show a handshake in the middle, and even use their green color. Now we have their name and their look on our cover. We knew this would be an issue, and that's exactly what we wanted.

How did we know? Several months earlier, I had the idea I'd write a book called *The Tipping Point of Networking*. I wrote to Malcolm Gladwell, author of *The Tipping Point*, asking for permission and even an endorsement. What I got back was a cease and desist letter from his attorney.

So, back to the story. We wrote the book, published 500 copies, distributed them to every Starbucks contact we had, and even Federal Expressed a gift-wrapped version to Howard Schultz to be delivered on his birthday. Genius!

Now that we'd blitzed our target and were armed with a book cover that used Starbucks's name and colors, and even a variation of their logo, we thought one of two things would happen.

They could buy the book. Back then, they had 16,000 stores. If they bought the book, say three books for each location, we were famous and on our way to being rich.

Or they could do what Malcolm Gladwell did and sic their attorneys on us. But this time, we'd be ready. If they chose to shut us down, we'd publish a press release we already had written. You'll love the headline: *Mega Coffee House Wants To Grind The Little Guy.*

Beautiful, yes?

So, if they buy the book, we're famous and on our way to being rich. If they don't buy the book, well, at least we can be famous. What went wrong?

We never anticipated and planned for the third option—they did nothing.

That's right, you have to be ready for people who will do nothing. Because most of the time, that's what people do. They do nothing.

And I've ended this book with this story for a very specific reason. You see, many people (like me) will read the last part of a book first. I don't know why, I just know they do. And if you are one of those last-part-first readers, I'm hoping the warning that most people do nothing is enough to get you to read the whole book.

You really can have Million Dollar Meetings. And using what I've learned and shared here, you can have many of them.

CHAPTER 29

If You Don't Act...

One night (actually it was a very early morning), I was on the front steps of the Hyatt Regency Hotel in Greenville, South Carolina. I was there for a Slazenger Company meeting. Don Swarat and I were regional account executives. It was raining, and my friend Don and I were wrapping up a very long night of entertaining the staff from the home office, warehouse, and sales teams.

If you've never been to a national meeting of a golf company, you need to know alcohol is involved. A lot of alcohol.

So there I sat looking up at Don standing in the rain. He had his tie wrapped around his head like Rambo, and we were discussing what had happened, what would happen, and world domination in general.

Then, Don posed a question. "What are you afraid of, Gouldy?"

I jokingly said, "Your breath tomorrow morning, Don."

And in a moment of sobriety among the drunkenness, Don said, "I'm afraid of regret."

It's not a chamber story, but it's a very important lesson I learned that night. And I try to never forget it or how it was intended.

Don wasn't warning me of the regret of failed action, he was warning me of the regret of inaction. He asked me, "What are you afraid of, Gouldy?" as we were discussing how successful our company could become.

Don would eventually become my boss. And he'd eventually fire me. He did it gently and with mercy. You see, Don knew I was dying as a Slazenger sales rep, having been demoted from being a regional account executive in a reorganization of the company.

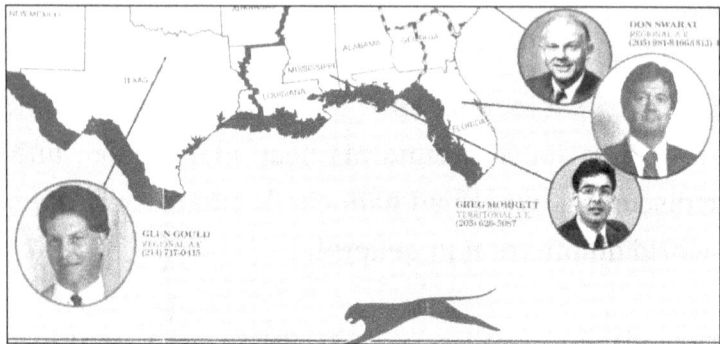

Slazenger staff promotional flyer 1987. Me far left.
Don Swarat far right.

But he also knew that I wasn't giving it what I could. I wasn't giving it my all. I wasn't all in.

And so, he fired me, and I deserved it. Because I was afraid to do something. I was afraid to do what needed to be done to ensure I would be successful. It wasn't that I didn't know what to do, it wasn't that I didn't know how to do it, it was that I was afraid to do it. I was afraid of the unknown.

Now, you know what to do. You know how to do it. And hopefully, you know what you want to do too.

So, go. Do something. Take this guide and use it to have your own Million Dollar Meetings. And when you do, I'd love to hear about it at Glen@MillionDollarMeetings.com.

You can be more, do more, have more, give more, and ultimately live more when you put yourself out there and meet people. They'll live more too because you did.

I wish for you the very best. But more importantly, I wish for you the courage to say what you want and to go after it with everything you have.

Be more. Do more. Have more. Give more. Live more.

Other titles by Glen Gould

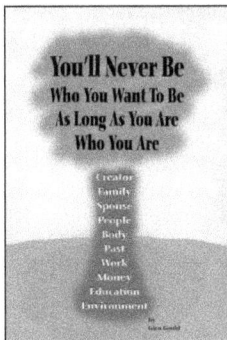

You'll Never Be Who You Want To Be As Long As You Are Who You Are by Glen Gould 2006 Inspiration Agents Press

Is Your Networking Working? by Glen Gould and Benjamin Turpin 2006 Inspiration Agents Press ISBN 987-0-9789985-0-9

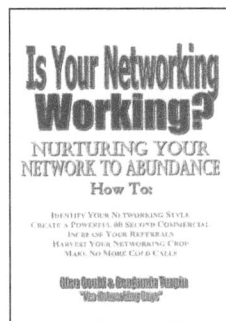

101 Networking Nuggets by Glen Gould and Benjamin Turpin 2006 Inspiration Agents Press ISBN 978-0-9789985-1-6

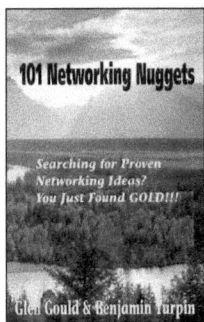

Meet Me At Starbucks by Ben Turpin and Glen Gould 2007 Inspiration Agents Press ISBN 978-0-9789985-5-4

Contact: Glen Gould
Glen@GlenGould.net
404.216.8881

187

www.ingramcontent.com/pod-product-compliance
Lightning Source LLC
Chambersburg PA
CBHW070401200326
41518CB00011B/2014